THE UNITED STATES TREASURY

Also by the authors

MOUNT VERNON
MONTICELLO
COSMONAUTS IN ORBIT
NORTH AND SOUTH KOREA
WOMEN ON THE MARCH
MARYLAND
UNIDENTIFIED FLYING OBJECTS

Also by Gene Gurney

AMERICA IN WAX
THE UNITED STATES COAST GUARD—A PICTORIAL HISTORY
THE OFFICIAL WASHINGTON, D.C., DIRECTORY: A PICTORIAL GUIDE
THE WAR IN THE AIR
A PICTORIAL HISTORY OF THE U.S. ARMY
HOW TO SAVE YOUR LIFE ON THE NATION'S HIGHWAYS AND BYWAYS
THE AIR FORCE MUSEUM

THE UNITED STATES TREASURY

A Pictorial History

Gene and Clare Gurney

CROWN PUBLISHERS, INC.   NEW YORK

Printed in the United States of America
Published simultaneously in Canada by General Publishing Company Limited

Designed by Jon M. Nelson

Library of Congress Cataloging in Publication Data

Gurney, Gene.
    The United States Treasury.
    Includes index.
    1.   United States.   Treasury Dept.—History—Pictorial
works.   I.   Gurney, Clare, joint author.   II.   Title.
HJ261.G87 1977   353.2   77-24767
ISBN 0-517-53099-6

Contents

2001143

"Most of the important measures of every government are connected with the Treasury Department."
ALEXANDER HAMILTON

Foreword

Almost two centuries have passed since the United States Congress declared that "there shall be a Department of the Treasury." But it was more than a decade earlier, during the Revolutionary War, that the Continental Congress faced the problem of raising funds to finance the war and manage the affairs of the Colonies. The Continental Congress, unlike our own, had no power to levy or collect taxes, so it chose the expedient of creating paper money which served as bills of credit. It was these sorts of problems that faced Alexander Hamilton when he assumed office as the first secretary of the treasury in 1789.

Sixty-three secretaries later—as I took office—the problems confronting me were in many ways like those of the first secretary of the treasury, intensified by the increased complexities of our finances, the vast growth of our country's population, and the grave responsibilities incumbent on the nation that freedom made the greatest on earth.

Treasury, with 110,000 employees, is not only one of the largest but one of the most influential Cabinet departments. Along with the State Department, it is also one of the two oldest Cabinet departments, and both were established in 1789. We are organized into the Office of the Secretary and eleven operating bureaus. While there are similarities in some of the general purposes of the Treasury bureaus, for the most part they have markedly different operating programs.

As Americans, we each have a responsibility to the future of our country, a responsibility that we can best understand if we have a knowledge of our past. Gene and Clare Gurney's book, covering the two-hundred-year history of the Treasury, helps us meet that responsibility and tells us why we can look forward with confidence to the future.

The Gurneys present, in a readable pictorial style, the story of the Treasury Department—the role it has played in our nation's history and the role it plays today in our national life, from collecting taxes to protecting the president. It's worthwhile reading for every citizen in this country.

William E. Simon
Secretary of the Treasury
January 14, 1977

"There Shall Be a Department of the Treasury"

THE FIRST CONGRESS TO CONVENE UNDER THE United States Constitution had been in session in New York for five months when, on September 2, 1789, it passed a bill that began with these words. "Be it enacted by the Senate and the House of Representatives of the United States of America in Congress assembled, that there shall be a Department of the Treasury." But the new republic had already had considerable experience with financial arrangements, arrangements made necessary by a chronic lack of money.

From the first days of the Revolutionary War the problem of obtaining funds had occupied much of the time of the former colonies' leaders who met in Philadelphia as the Continental Congress. Unfortunately, Congress had no power to levy and collect taxes; nor was there any tangible basis upon which to seek credit abroad from other nations or from foreign money interests. The delegates, therefore, adopted the expedient, but precarious, course of creating paper money in the form of bills of credit, or promises to pay, pledging redemption in coin at some later date. Their constituents, imbued by the justice of the Revolutionary cause, approved, although they

Alexander Hamilton, the first secretary of the treasury, as he appears in the painting by C. L. Ransom that now hangs in the office of the secretary of the treasury.

had already experienced the consequences of depreciated colonial currencies. On July 23, 1775, only a few days after the Battle of Bunker Hill, the Congress appointed Richard Bache, Stephen Pascall, and Michael Hillegas to superintend the printing of $2 million worth of bills, and twenty-eight citizens of Philadelphia were employed to sign and number them.

On July 29, 1775, the Continental Congress fixed the responsibility for managing the finances of the Revolutionary government upon two treasurers and chose Michael Hillegas and George Clymer to fill the posts. As joint treasurers for the United Colonies, Hillegas and Clymer were required to live in Philadelphia and to post bonds of $100,000 each to ensure the "faithful performance of their office." Later that year Congress ordered a census for the purpose of allocating the burden of the public debt among the thirteen former colonies and at the same time arranged for the printing of another $2 million in paper money.

The weak economic structure of the United Colonies now engaging the well-equipped, and presumably all-powerful, British forces demanded the most efficient possible handling of public finances. Accordingly, on Febuary 17, 1776, a committee composed of James Duane, Elbridge Gerry, Richard Smith, Thomas Nelson, and Thomas Willing was designated to superintend the Treasury, examine the accounts, and report periodically to Congress. An additional $4 million in bills was authorized.

Continuing in its attempts to establish a workable system of managing its funds, Congress next established a Treasury Office of Accounts under the supervision of the Treasury Committee and directed that an auditor general and a competent corps of assistants and clerks be appointed. In the opinion of the legislators: "Nothing is of greater consequence than that the public records should be regularly stated and kept and justly liquidated and settled." Accounts and claims against the United Colonies were to be presented to the Treasury Office, which was to handle all the government's contracts, securities, and obligations. Congress further provided that colonial assemblies, conventions, councils, committees of safety, paymasters, and officers of the military would, at the request of the committee, submit their accounts to the Treasury Office together with any data that would be of assistance in "settling and adjusting most fairly the public accounts." This was the shape of its financial establishment when the newborn republic proclaimed its Declaration of Independence to the world on July 4, 1776.

Now endowed with national status, the United States entered the credit market as a borrower. In the autumn of 1776 the Treasury Committee recommended the raising of "five hundred thousand dollars for the use of the United States." Congress agreed and fixed the rate of interest at 4 percent per annum. The faith of the United States was pledged, loan offices were established in each state, and commissioners appointed to manage them. The commissioners received the proceeds of the loans and forwarded them to the Treasury of the United States. Each commissioner retained one-eighth of 1 percent of what he took in to cover the costs of transacting the business of his office.

During the war years the *Congressional Journal* carried reports of new Treasury Committee appointments, recommendations for punishing counterfeiters, suggestions for protecting valid loan certificates, an order to remove the Treasury Office to York, Pennsylvania, when the enemy came too close to Philadelphia, and plans for a Treasury reorganization as its fiscal functions increased. Every possible means of obtaining revenue was considered, including a lot-

tery scheme undertaken in November 1776, which failed to attract enough subscribers.

Michael Hillegas became treasurer of the United States on September 6, 1777, a post he held during the entire pre-Constitution period. George Clymer had resigned as joint treasurer in August 1776, to sit in Congress (his name later appears several times as a member of the Treasury Committee), and no one was named to replace him. Congress, meanwhile, devoted Tuesdays, Thursdays, and Saturdays to Treasury and finance matters.

A reorganization of the Treasury in 1778 provided for an auditor and two chambers of accounts to examine and pass upon all accounts and claims against the government, a comptroller who kept the Treasury seal and affixed it to all accounts and vouchers payable to or by the United States, and a treasurer upon whom the comptroller drew and who kept all monies and loan certificates.

In February 1779, Congress established an office of the secretary of the treasury and appointed Robert

Philadelphia merchant Michael Hillegas, who became treasurer of the United States in 1777. He held that office until Congress established the Department of the Treasury in 1789.

Troup to the post. However, this office (along with the comptroller's) was abolished that July when a Board of the Treasury supplanted the Treasury Committee and took over the seal. The Treasury Board consisted of five commissioners, two of whom were members of Congress. The noncongressional commissioners were to be elected annually, the congressional members every six months. The board was charged with general supervision of finances, estimating public expenses, maintaining watch on public accounts, and ensuring that debtors were brought to account and that frauds against the Treasury were detected.

Both the Board of the Treasury and the Treasury Office ceased to function in September 1781, when Robert Morris of Pennsylvania, a signer of the Declaration of Independence, took office as superintendent of finance. That position had been set up to handle financial matters in February 1781, as part of a congressional plan to give executive responsibilities to single department heads.

"Financier" Morris was widely respected for his business acumen, especially his ability to deliver money and food quickly on emergency call from General Washington. His duties as superintendent of finance, as outlined by Congress, would require all his expertise: "To examine into the state of the public debt, the public expenditures, and the public revenue; to digest and report plans for improving and regulating the finances, and for establishing order and economy in the expenditure of public money; to direct the execution of all plans which shall be adopted by Congress respecting revenue and expenditures; to superintend and control all persons employed in procuring supplies for the public service and in the expenditure of public money; to obtain accounts of all the issues of the specific supplies furnished by the several states; to compel the payment of all monies due the United States, and in his official character (or in such manner as the laws of the respective states shall direct) to prosecute on behalf of the United States for all delinquencies (respecting

In this drawing George Washington (seated, right) is conferring with Robert Morris (seated, left) and Alexander Hamilton, probably about the financial problems of the newly formed government.

Robert Morris, who served as superintendent of finance from 1781 until 1789.

the public revenues and expenditures); to report to Congress the officers which shall be necessary for assisting him in the various branches of the department."

Although the busy Mr. Morris was managing both the Treasury and the navy (Congress had failed to name an agent of the marine), the Treasury prospered under his care. On June 17, 1783, these words of praise appeared in the *Congressional Journal*: "It appears the business of that office [superintendent of finance] has been conducted with great ability and assiduity, in a manner highly advantageous to the United States, and in conformity with the system laid down by Congress; that since the appointment of the Superintendent of Finance the public accounts of receipts and expenditures have been regularly and punctually kept; that many of the accounts which preceded this institution have already been settled and most of the others put into a train of adjustment."

Morris remained in office until May 1784 when ill health forced his resignation. He was replaced by three commissioners who made up a Board of the Treasury that Congress established to "superintend the Treasury and manage the finances of the United States." The board administered Treasury functions until September 1789.

The inspiration for the old Treasury seal pictured here is unknown, although it may have been the watchdog purchased by the Philadelphia mint in 1793, the year the mint began coining money.

Until the design was changed in 1968, this was the official Treasury seal. The Latin inscription translates: Seal of the Treasury of North America. The scales represent those held by the blind Goddess of Justice, the stars stand for the thirteen original colonies, and the key is a heraldic device denoting offices of state.

The Act to Establish the Treasury Department, which the United States Congress passed on September 2, 1789, provided for a secretary of the treasury, who would be in charge of the department; a comptroller; an auditor; a treasurer; a register; and an assistant to the secretary of the treasury, appointed by the secretary.

To the secretary of the treasury, Congress allotted such vital tasks as planning for the improvement of the republic's revenue and managing it for the support of the public credit, preparing estimates of the public revenue and expenditures, overseeing the collection of the revenue, developing the forms that would be needed to conduct the Treasury's business and keep its records, issuing warrants for monies to be paid from the Treasury, performing certain functions relative to the sale of public lands, and reporting regularly to Congress on Treasury matters.

Congress concluded the Act to Establish the Treasury Department by stipulating: "And be it further inacted, That no person appointed to any office instituted by this Act shall directly or indirectly be concerned or interested in carrying on the business of trade or commerce, or be the owner in whole or in part of any sea vessel, or purchase by himself, or another in trust for him, any public lands or other public property; or be concerned in the purchase or disposal of any public securities of any state, or of the United States, or take or apply to his own use, any emolument or gain for negotiating or transacting any business in the said department, other than what shall be allowed by law, and if any person shall offend against any of the prohibitions of this Act, he shall be deemed guilty of a high misdemeanor, and forfeit to the United States the penalty of three thousand dollars, and shall upon conviction be removed from office, and forever thereafter incapable of holding any office under the United States."

President Washington's choice for secretary of the treasury was his former aide-de-camp, Alexander Hamilton, a prominent New York lawyer who had actively participated in the framing of the Constitution.

Born in the West Indies, Hamilton left home for New York when he was sixteen. As a student at King's College (now Columbia University), he wrote several pamphlets defending the colonies in their quarrel with the British government. In 1776 he left King's College to join a New York artillery company, which became part of the Continental forces. After taking part in military engagements in New York and at Trenton and Princeton in New Jersey, Hamilton became General Washington's aide-de-camp with the rank of lieutenant colonel. He served as Washington's principal assistant until the closing days of the war when, as commander of a light infantry brigade, he participated in the fighting that led to the British surrender at Yorktown.

After the war the future secretary of the treasury studied law. He also began to take an active part in politics as an advocate of a strong central government. His political beliefs, along with those of James Madison and John Jay, found expression in a series of essays defending the Constitution, which are credited with persuading several doubtful states to ratify that document.

Hamilton had been one of those who urged the reluctant George Washington to become president of the United States, and his former aide-de-camp was

The bronze statue of Alexander Hamilton by James Earl Fraser that stands at the foot of the Treasury's south steps.

Albert Gallatin, the distinguished fourth secretary of the treasury, is represented by a statue, also by Fraser, at the Treasury's north entrance.

When the U.S. government moved from Philadelphia in 1800, the sixty-nine employees of the Treasury set up shop in this building, which they shared with the seven-member staff of the State Department and a few employees of the navy. The building housed the Treasury Department until 1814 when the British burned it to the ground.

Louis McLane, who was secretary at the time the Treasury building burned down in 1833.

the third man that Washington selected for his cabinet. Thirty-two years old when he took the oath of office on September 11, 1789, the first secretary of the treasury favored a stable banking system, sound currency, and a simplified and centralized system of government purchasing.

From the beginning of his stewardship, Hamilton applied himself to the careful execution of the duties assigned to his office by Congress, attending personally to such minute details as devising official Treasury forms. He devoted much of his time and attention to organizing and expanding the work of the Customs collectors, customs duties being the main source of funds of the federal government. Shortly after taking office, the secretary approached the collectors of customs for their ideas on using boats to protect the revenue from smugglers, both foreign and domestic, who were landing "spiritous liquors," rum, wine, molasses, tea, sugar, nails, candles, leather, and numerous other products without paying an import duty to the Treasury. Moreover, some foreign ships were engaging in coastwise trade, which was reserved for the fledgling merchant marine. By the summer of the following year Congress had authorized a Revenue Marine of ten cutters, thereby creating the first seagoing branch of the United States military forces. It flourishes today as the United States Coast Guard.

Hamilton's first report to Congress, a historic document, illustrates his belief in the importance of sound fiscal policies in the development of the nation. In the report the secretary wrote: "States, like individuals who observe their engagements, are respected and trusted. Every breach of public engagement, whether by choice or necessity, is hurtful to the public credit." He continued to expound his theories with these statements: "Those who are most commonly creditors of a nation are, generally speaking, enlightened men." "The debt of the United States . . . was the price of liberty. . . . The faith of America was pledged for it, and with solemnities that give peculiar force to the obligation. . . . While the observance of that good faith which is the basis of the public credit is recommended by the strongest inducements of political expediency, it is enforced by consideration of still greater authority, the immutable principles of moral obligation."

Before he resigned from the Treasury in 1795 to return to his law practice, Hamilton had persuaded Congress to acknowledge all United States debt, including obligations incurred by the states during the Revolutionary War. As confidence grew in the nation's integrity, creditors were encouraged to exchange their old bonds for new issues. The opening of the Bank of the United States, jointly owned and managed by the government and private investors, further improved the financial situation.

Today a bronze statue of the first secretary of the treasury stands at the foot of the south steps of the Treasury building in Washington. One side of the pedestal carries this inscription:

Alexander Hamilton
1757–1804
First Secretary of the Treasury
Soldier   Orator   Statesman
Champion of Constitutional Union
Representative Government and
National Integrity

A tribute by Daniel Webster has been inscribed on the opposite side: "He smote the rock of the national resources and abundant streams of revenue gushed forth. He touched the dead corpse of public credit and it sprung up on its feet."

During the first years of the republic the Treasury was quartered in Philadelphia, the temporary capital. When the seat of government was removed to Washington in 1800, a small wooden structure designed by English architect George Hatfield and located on the northeast corner of the present building was provided for the Treasury. It was partially destroyed by fire in 1801, repaired, and occupied by the department until the British burned it to the ground when they attacked Washington in 1814.

During the years between 1801 and 1814 the Swiss-born Albert Gallatin was secretary of the treasury. His appointment, by Thomas Jefferson, followed several years in Congress during which he developed an interest in government fiscal operations. As Treasury secretary, Gallatin espoused debt reduction, specific appropriations, and strict accountability for government funds. He was well on the way to achieving his goals when the War of 1812 created new financial problems for the United States.

Gallatin remained in Washington for several months to arrange war financing, then sailed for Europe on a peace mission. At the time of the Treasury fire he had resigned from his post as secretary to take a leading role in the negotiations that brought the war to an end. Gallatin became United States minister to France and, later, to England. Returning to private life in 1827, he entered banking in New York.

The Treasury building as it appeared in 1855. The small building on the right housed the State Department. The Treasury building erected in 1817 and destroyed by fire in 1833 was almost identical to the State Department's building.

Other than the building itself, losses sustained by the Treasury in the 1814 fire appear to have been minor. In answer to a congressional request for information, Secretary of the Treasury Alexander J. Dallas wrote: "In obedience to the resolution of the House of Representatives of the 24 inst., the Secretary of the Treasury respectfully reports: That, with the exception of some old letters from the collectors of the customs and commissioners of loans and other unimportant documents, no loss of official books or papers was sustained by his particular office by reason of the incursion of the enemy in the month of August, 1814."

Treasurer of the United States Thomas T. Tucker was able to assure Congress: "Ledgers, journals, remittances, bank, draft, and other books generally, in use since the year 1810, have been preserved, and many from the first establishment of the Treasury, particularly all the payments and receipts on account of the Treasury, War and Navy Departments." He added that "many of the books and papers destroyed were brought from Philadelphia and very few could ever have been wanted."

A building erected during the reconstruction that followed the departure of the British housed the Treasury until 1833 when it too was destroyed by fire. And this time the department suffered a considerable loss.

Secretary Louis McLane reported in a circular dated April 12, 1833: "In the late conflagration of

Secretary of the Treasury James Guthrie (1853–1857) is credited with reforming the administration of the department.

the Treasury building nearly all the correspondence of the Secretary of the Treasury, from the establishment of the Department to the 31st of March, 1833, was destroyed; including, as well the original letters and communications addressed to the Secretary of the Treasury, as the records of the letters and communications written by him."

In another report McLane discussed the origin of the fire: "From all that has hitherto transpired, it does not appear that the disaster is attributable to any particular neglect or inattention on the part of those who had charge of the building. It is shewn that past ten o'clock at night all the fires were in a safe condition, and that no lights of any kind had been used in that part of the building in which the fire originated. Though the person employed to watch that night was asleep when the fire was discovered, it appears that it was not considered his duty to be awake all night, and that, in fact, it has been the authorized practice for many years, for the watchmen in the building to lie down to sleep after ten or eleven o'clock. No satisfactory proof has been obtained of the cause of the disaster."

Later, however, an investigation authorized by President Andrew Jackson led to the arrest of two brothers who were charged with setting the fire to destroy papers that would have incriminated several persons employed as Treasury agents. One brother was finally acquitted after four trials, but the other was sentenced to ten years in prison.

With the papers, books, and other records that had been salvaged from the burning building, the secretary and his staff moved into temporary quarters. To guard against another conflagration and to protect Treasury property, McLane appointed one J. P. Pepper to the post of superintendent of the building.

The secretary outlined Superintendent Pepper's duties:

You will carefully inspect each building, in company with the Messenger having charge of it, and will see that the fires are extinguished and the building properly secured, and if you discover any negligence yourself you will promptly report the same to the Secretary. One of the Messengers of the office, occupying each building will attend at 6 o'clock in the morning and receive the key of the same from the watchman, and the buildings will remain in charge of its messenger until 6 o'clock in the evening, when the keys will be delivered to the watchman. The watchmen will be provided with a safe lamp, which is to be kept during the night in some secure place. Two watchmen will remain in the building from 6 in the evening until 6 in the morning. It is not required that they should remain awake after 11 o'clock, but they will take care to be in a situation to be easily alarmed, and ready to afford any assistance which the safety of the building may require. Where they have taken charge they will not quit the building until properly relieved. A military guard having been provided, sentinels will be stationed in the front and rear of the building from 6 o'clock in the evening until 6 o'clock in the morning.

You will provide suitable fire ladders, not less than four in number, to be kept conveniently and in readiness for use, and also not less than ten fire buckets for each building, and the proper quantity office hose, and such other articles as may be necessary in case of fire. You will also make arrangements with the Company having charge of the nearest Engine belonging to the United States for keeping it constantly ready, and for bringing it promptly to the building in case of fire.

You will cause 3 lamps and 2 sentry boxes to be provided and put up. It will be a part of your duty to provide fuel and oil, and other articles necessary for the building, and see that the fuel be safely put away. You will see that the entire premises are kept in a clean and becoming order. As these buildings do not belong to the United States no fixtures or permanent improvements or repairs will be added by you without the sanction of the Secretary of the Treasury. You will occasionally visit the buildings at night to see that the sentries and watchmen are vigilant and careful, and that the buildings are safe. The Messengers, laborers and watchmen, will all be subject to your direction as far as may be necessary to the execution of your duties.

Having arranged for the security of his temporary quarters, Secretary McLane campaigned for a new, fireproof Treasury building. He recommended a structure "of sufficient extent to accommodate all the public offices under the same roof, having regard as well to those already organized as those which the growth of the country will probably render necessary for some years to come."

President James Buchanan (seated, right) *was visiting the construction site of the Treasury Department's new south wing when this photo was taken in 1857. With the president are Secretary of the Treasury James Guthrie, the Treasury architect, and the labor foreman.*

Construction is under way on the Treasury's south wing. On the right, Pennsylvania Avenue stretches eastward to the Capitol, which has not yet acquired its dome.

In this 1859 photo building materials surround the new south wing.

Construction of the south wing is nearing completion. The builders finished their work in September 1861.

"Treasury girls" are leaving work on a rainy Washington evening in this sketch by A. R. Ward. During the Civil War the Treasury's Bureau of Engraving and Printing hired hundreds of women clerks for jobs usually performed by men.

In a photo taken during the Civil War, the Treasury building looks out over a pasture where cattle are grazing (the present site of the Department of Commerce building). The top of the White House can be seen to the left of the Treasury.

A sketch by Albert Berghaus depicts President Andrew Johnson (seated, left) meeting with his Cabinet in the third-floor Treasury building office that the president used while waiting for Mrs. Lincoln to move from the White House after President Lincoln's assassination.

President Johnson (center) holds a reception for ambassadors in a room at the Treasury Department that is draped in mourning for President Abraham Lincoln. The sketch of the reception, held on April 20, 1865, is by Albert Berghaus.

Three years after the Treasury fire Congress passed legislation authorizing a new fireproof building. It was to be erected near the site of the original Treasury building and be large enough to take care of the "present and future accommodations of the Treasury Department." Congress recommended the "material of which the walls of the Capitol and President's mansion are constructed . . . provided, upon full inquiry, a cheaper and more suitable material cannot be obtained," and the legislators further stipulated: "The foundation walls below the surface of the earth and two feet above shall be of the hardest and most solid rock." The sum of $100,000 was appropriated for construction.

It is generally agreed that the original plan called for placing the new Treasury building where it would not obstruct the mile and a half of Pennsylvania Avenue that stretched from the Capitol to the White House, but that is exactly what happened. First, however, time passed without a final decision. At this point legend takes over. According to a story that has gained wide circulation over the years, President Andrew Jackson became impatient with the delay in choosing a site for the Treasury. One morning he is said to have left the White House accompanied by members of his staff. Upon reaching the vacant building site, the president examined it. Then, planting his cane near the northeast corner, he declared: "Right here is where I want the cornerstone laid!"

Whether or not Jackson uttered those words, Robert Mills, who designed the building finally erected, is on record as assuring a congressional committee that its "precise location" had been determined by the "positive directions of the late President."

The selection of a site was only one of the problems that plagued the Treasury's building project. Work was already underway when the Congressional Committee on Public Buildings and Grounds issued a report criticizing the location and plan of the building and the material that was being used in its construction. Moreover, the committee submitted a draft of a bill calling for the demolition of the partially completed structure. Construction was suspended, then resumed. Finally, in 1831, enough progress had been made to allow Secretary of the Treasury Levi Woodbury to move in along with the

Hugh McCulloch, secretary of the treasury from 1865 until 1869. He had previously been the Treasury's first comptroller of the currency.

register, the comptroller, and other Treasury officials. The attorney general of the United States also occupied an office in the still unfinished building.

Something less than $700,000 had been spent when the Treasury building was completed in 1842. The structure contained 150 rooms, not enough, as it turned out, to accommodate the expanding business of the Treasury.

In 1855 Congress appropriated $300,000 to enlarge the Treasury. A south wing was opened in 1861, a west wing in 1864 and, in 1869, a north wing. Total costs approached $6 million when the north wing was completed and the Treasury building assumed its present form.

An imposing structure, centered on an interior court, the Treasury building covers more than 120,000 square feet of ground at the southwest corner of 15th Street and Pennsylvania Avenue. Its Greek Revival design is said to be one of the finest examples of this style in Washington.

Seventy-two magnificent Ionic columns adorn the facades of the Treasury building. Thirty-four of the thirty-six-foot-high pillars are located on the east, or 15th Street, side of the building; eighteen are on the west side, ten on the north side, and ten on the south side. The building's main entrance faces 15th Street, although the Treasury Place entrance on the south or, possibly, the west entrance looking across to the

White House, may have been intended for that honor. Convenience to transportation and to Washington's business district encouraged the use of the 15th Street entrance, which leads to the ground floor of the five-story building.

Executive offices occupy most of today's Treasury building, but, despite its size, only 10 percent of the Treasury's Washington staff can be accommodated. As a result, Treasury activities have expanded into an annex and some twenty other buildings. The secretary of the treasury occupies a suite on the third floor of the main Treasury building. At the north end of the building is the historic, two-story-high Cash Room, so named because until 1976 United States government checks could be exchanged for cash there. In 1869 President Grant held his inaugural ball in the splendor of the Cash Room, where the walls, window frames, and doors are of solid marble.

Fifteen vaults, ranging in size from 10 by 16 feet to 50 by 90 feet, occupy the Treasury building's basement. At one time the vaults held most of the nation's gold and silver bullion. Now, however, they store coins, currency, bonds, and securities. Combination and time locks safeguard the vaults. In addition, they are equipped with an electrical protection system that alerts the captain of the guard, the Secret Service and Washington's police headquarters. The Treasury basement also houses a pistol range used by Secret Service and other enforcement personnel to maintain marksmanship.

One of the giant columns that decorate the facade of the north wing of the Treasury building was being lifted into place when this photo was taken.

During World War II the Treasury basement contained a shelter area for use by the president if it should become necessary. A tunnel connected the wartime White House with the shelter, which would also have served as a refuge for the president's Cabinet.

Most of the offices authorized in the legislation creating the Treasury Department are still in existence. However, in some cases functions with little fiscal significance have been transferred to more appropriate agencies. The Treasury, for instance, supervised the Postal Service until 1829; from 1812 to 1849 the General Land Office (now in the Interior Department) was in the Treasury; operations associated with business were Treasury activities before the Department of Commerce and Labor was established in 1903. The collection of fees from masters or owners of sailing vessels for the care and treatment of American seamen, originally assigned to Collectors of Customs, developed into the Marine Hospital Service, parent of the Public Health Service, which eventually took over enforcement of regulations for the prevention of the introduction and spread of communicable disease, supervision of the National Quarantine Service, and research in public health and hygiene. The Public Health Service became part of the Federal Security Agency in 1939, and was transferred to the Department of Health, Education and Welfare in 1953.

For many years the Department of the Treasury supervised the construction of federal buildings.

Another view of the Treasury building's north wing under construction.

This function, the responsibility of the Treasury's supervising architect, was transferred in 1939 to the Federal Works Agency and moved to the General Services Administration in 1949. In 1967 the Coast Guard was transferred from the Treasury to the Department of Transportation. One year later the Bureau of Narcotics was moved to the Department of Justice where it became the Bureau of Narcotics and Dangerous Drugs. Duties assigned by the original Treasury legislation to a comptroller and to an auditor are now the responsibility of the General Accounting Office.

But succeeding congresses and presidents, while transferring some functions from the Treasury, have charged it with other responsibilities. In order to execute its manifold duties the department now maintains offices in most of the nation's principal cities. In addition, Treasury representatives are on duty at United States embassies in the major world capitals.

This drawing of the Treasury was made from the southeast corner of the building.

A drawing by an unidentified artist of the secretary's office in the Treasury building as it appeared in 1867 during the incumbency of Hugh McCulloch.

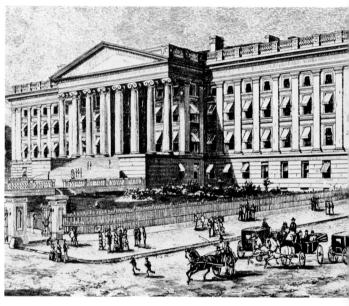

A drawing showing guests arriving at the entrance to the north wing of the Treasury building for President Grant's inaugural ball on March 4, 1869.

A few years after President Grant's inaugural ball an artist made this drawing of the south and west wings of the Treasury. The building has much the same appearance today.

The Cash Room's two-story-high lobby. At one time the narrow gallery on the second-floor level was open to the public.

President Grant's inaugural ball was held in the Treasury's ornate Cash Room, pictured here after it had reverted to its role as a bank within the Treasury building. During the inaugural festivities bands played in the Cash Room and several other parts of the building. Two thousand ball invitations each admitted a gentleman and two ladies. The resulting crush caused ladies to faint and many guests could not get within sight of the refreshments.

A closer look at the décor of the Cash Room, reported to be the most expensive room in the world at the time of its construction.

In this photo taken during the 1920s Cash Room customers wait to transact business at the cashier's window.

The Cash Room in 1965. The Treasury Department continued to provide free government check cashing service in the Cash Room until 1976. The elaborately decorated room is now used for conferences.

One of the doors leading to the Cash Room.

In the days when many men chewed tobacco, the Treasury maintained a cuspidor washing and sterilizing room.

The Treasury's carpentry shop.

This photo, taken at about the time of World War I, shows horse-drawn wagons and one of the new horseless carriages (at right) *waiting at the Treasury's 15th Street entrance for a currency shipment.*

The Treasury's finest team of horses pulled the secretary's carriage, shown here with its liveried driver and footman.

Since the establishment of the department in 1789, the secretary of the treasury has been the second-ranking member of the president's Cabinet and his chief adviser on fiscal affairs. Chief executives, beginning with George Washington, have called upon the sixty-four men who have occupied the office of secretary of the treasury for advice on domestic and international financial policies, tax matters, and the management of the public debt.

In addition to serving as adviser to the president, the secretary of the treasury supervises the operation of an executive department whose activities range from law enforcement to coin and currency manufacture to service as the government's financial agent. He submits an annual report to Congress on the state of United States finances and supplies other information on Treasury operations that Congress may request.

The secretary represents the United States on the governing boards of the Internationl Monetary Fund, the International Bank for Reconstruction and Development, the Inter-American Development Bank, and the Asian Development Bank.

Treasury officers, who, like the secretary himself, are appointed by the president with the approval of the Senate, assist the secretary in carrying out his duties. A deputy secretary is responsible for the general supervision and direction of the Treasury Department. As second in command, he acts for the secretary in the latter's absence, sickness, or unavailability.

The secretary of the treasury receives advice and assistance from his undersecretary for monetary affairs whose responsibilities include the development of Treasury policies in the areas of international monetary affairs, domestic fiscal and economic matters, trade, energy, and the management of the public debt. He is the third ranking official in the department.

International financial, economic, and monetary policies and programs are the special responsibility of the assistant secretary for international affairs. The assistant secretary for capital investment and debt management advises the secretary of the treasury and the undersecretary for monetary affairs on those subjects and various financing programs. United States

During the 1920s the Treasury's horse-drawn vehicles gave way to a fleet of trucks.

economic policies and programs are the province of the assistant secretary for economic policy. He deals with production, price and market trends, and the administration of gold and silver regulations. A fiscal assistant secretary, whom he appoints, helps the secretary of the treasury administer the department's financing operations, which include the investment of trust and other accounts, supervising the cash position of the Treasury, and acting as liaison between the secretary and other agencies in financial matters.

An undersecretary of the treasury advises and assists the secretary and the deputy secretary with the management of the department, tariff and law enforcement matters, relations with Congress, and the Treasury's coin and currency manufacturing function. Three assistant secretaries share these responsibilities with the undersecretary.

Another officer who assists the secretary of the treasury is the treasurer of the United States who reviews currency production and redemption, signs currency, promotes the sale of United States savings bonds, and acts as a spokesman for the Department of the Treasury.

Each of the Treasury's operating bureaus and divisions has its own executive who carries out his duties under the general supervision of one of the assistant secretaries of the Treasury. It is the operating bureaus and divisions that carry out the financial, law-enforcement, tax, coin-and-currency-manufacturing, and other functions of the Treasury that affect the life of every American.

One of the Treasury's second-floor halls in a photo taken sometime prior to 1959. The fluted, cast-iron pilasters are still there, but the ornate open elevators have been replaced by self-operating cars.

A century's accumulation of grime was removed during the cleaning of the Treasury building in 1954. An earlier cleaning project in 1903 was halted because critics said it was destroying the "antique look" of the building.

The massive thirty-six-ton door that safeguards the Treasury's main vault.

Prior to 1958 the Treasury building carried no name. Here workmen are lettering "The Treasury Department" on the south portico. Alexander Hamilton's statue is in the foreground.

This photograph shows the Treasury's south portico as it appears from Pershing Square. Seated on the bench are Mrs. Lyndon Johnson and Nash Castro of the National Park Service.

The office of the treasurer of the United States on the second floor of the Treasury building.

Secretary of the Treasury John W. Snyder (1946–1953) poses with some of his top assistants beneath a portrait of Secretary of the Treasury Albert Gallatin (1801–1814). From left: General Counsel Thomas J. Lynch, Assistant Secretary William McC. Martin, Jr., Under Secretary Edward H. Foley, Jr., Secretary Snyder, Assistant Secretary John S. Graham, Fiscal Assistant Secretary Edward F. Bartelt, and Administrative Assistant William W. Parsons.

In 1950 Secretary Snyder spoke at the dedication of the Treasury's Liberty Bell, one of fifty-odd reproductions cast in France for display in the United States in connection with the $653,950,000 Savings Bond Independence Drive.

Secretary of the Treasury George P. Shultz (seated, right) and Mikolai S. Patolichev, USSR minister of foreign trade (seated, left), are signing a treaty designed to promote economic and cultural relations between the United States and the Soviet Union by eliminating tax barriers. Shultz was secretary of the treasury from 1972 until 1974.

On October 18, 1972, Secretary of the Treasury Shultz (standing, left) represented the Treasury Department at the ceremony designating the Treasury as a National Historic Landmark. The citation read: "This site possesses exceptional value in commemorating or illustrating the history of the United States." Seated in the front row to the right of the lectern are Secretary of the Interior Rogers Morton and Mrs. Richard Nixon.

The Treasury's south portico during the colorful landmark ceremony.

Secretary of the Treasury William E. Simon, who succeeded Secretary Shultz in 1974, and Saudi Arabian Finance Minister Aba al-Khail sign a financial agreement as representatives of their countries.

NOW SPEAKING

THE GOVERNOR FOR UNITED STATES

Secretary Simon addresses the assembly of the International Monetary Fund. The secretary represented the United States on the fund's board of governors.

Secretary William E. Simon discusses a public affairs release with his press secretary, Robert E. Nipp, during the Arab oil embargo (October 17, 1973–March 13, 1974). To solve the energy shortage caused by the embargo, Secretary Simon formed the Federal Energy Office (later the Federal Energy Administration) on December 4, 1973, and served as the head of the agency until April 13, 1974. This was in addition to his duties as secretary of the treasury. As "Energy Czar," he allocated the available fuel around the country in such a manner as to soften the impact on jobs—he kept the "wheels of industry running." (Photo by Dennis Brack, Black Star)

Secretary W. Michael Blumenthal's office on the third floor of the Treasury building. Blumenthal became secretary of the treasury in 1977.

President Jimmy Carter (left) visits the main Treasury building, next door to the White House, early in his administration. Treasury Secretary Blumenthal shares a press conference with the president in the Cash Room on this occasion.

Secretary Blumenthal (left) signs an official Treasury Department document with his executive assistant, Bernard Winograd, looking on.

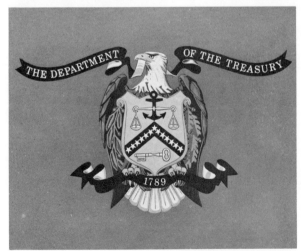

The official flag of the Department of the Treasury. The flag's background is mint leaf green; the shield has a yellow background with brown outlines.

The official Treasury seal today.

Azie T. Morton, who became the thirty-sixth treasurer of the United States in 1977.

This photo of a government wine-testing laboratory was taken
when the regulation of the alcohol industry was the responsibility
of the Bureau of Internal Revenue. ATF continues to test alcoholic beverages to ensure that the consumer gets what he pays for
and that alcoholic beverages do not contain harmful ingredients.

Special Controls for Special Industries: The Bureau of Alcohol, Tobacco and Firearms

BECAUSE THE ALCOHOL, TOBACCO, FIREARMS AND explosives industries pose special problems of law enforcement, regulation, and tax collection, the Treasury Department's newest operating bureau deals exclusively with them.

Although the Bureau of Alcohol, Tobacco and Firearms was officially established only in 1972, the federal government became involved in some of its functions as early as 1791 when Congress levied the first tax on distilled spirits. As amended in 1792, that pioneer internal revenue statute called for a tax of 54¢ on the per gallon capacity of each still, or, alternatively, 7¢ on each gallon of whiskey produced by the still. The tax, which was collected at the stills where the spirits were manufactured, proved to be so unpopular that, in 1794, seven thousand protestors staged an angry demonstration in western Pennsylvania. One of their leaders was Albert Gallatin who later became the fourth secretary of the treasury. To put down the Whiskey Rebellion, President George Washington had to send fifteen thousand militiamen into Pennsylvania from other states, an action that established an important precedent for federal enforcement of federal laws.

Calling liquor taxes "infernal" and "hostile to the genius of a free people," President Thomas Jefferson abolished the excises in 1802. But in 1812 Secretary of the Treasury Albert Gallatin, his days as a leader of the Whiskey Rebellion now behind him, had to recommend to Congress that liquor taxes be reinstated to help pay for the war with Britain that began that year. The levies were again abolished in 1817 and not revived until 1861 when revenue had to be raised for Civil War expenses.

Collecting the tax on spirits continued to be difficult. In 1863 George Boutwell, the newly appointed commissioner of internal revenue, found it necessary to hire three detectives to combat the illegal production of whiskey, which was depriving the government of income needed for the army. These detectives can be considered the precursors of the agents who worked for the Internal Revenue Service's Alcohol, Tobacco and Firearms Division and their successors, the agents of today's Bureau of Alcohol, Tobacco and Firearms.

After the Civil War the Bureau of Internal Revenue continued to collect taxes on alcoholic beverages and to enforce laws prohibiting illegal traffic in liquor. The latter became particularly important after the ratification of the 18th, or Prohibition, Amendment in 1919. The repeal of the amendment in 1933 again legalized the manufacture, transportation, and sale of alcoholic beverages. Although "moonshining," or trafficking in unlawfully distilled whiskey, diminished with the end of Prohibition, it did not disappear, and the problem of collecting

31

Armed insurrection during the Whiskey Rebellion flared up in western Pennsylvania. This cartoon, depicting a tax collector being "tarred and feathered and run out of town on a rail," became the most famous cartoon of the period and coined a new expression, which lives today.

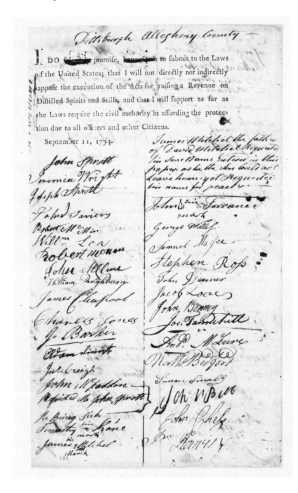

taxes on legal spirits remained. Both came under the jurisdiction of the Alcohol Tax Unit (ATU), which was set up in the Bureau of Internal Revenue to enforce tax laws affecting industrial alcohol, distilled spirits, wine, and beer.

In 1941 ATU agents began to investigate violations of the National Firearms Act of 1934 and the Federal Firearms Act of 1938, legislation designed to control machine guns and sawed-off shotguns, the weapons most frequently used in organized crime.

When the collection of taxes on tobacco products was added to ATU's responsibilities in 1951, the agency became the Alcohol and Tobacco Tax Division within the Bureau of Internal Revenue. Another increase in responsibilities and another name change, to Alcohol, Tobacco and Firearms Division, followed the passage, in 1968, of the Gun Control Act and the Omnibus Crime Control and Safe Streets Act. In 1970 the division extended its activities to include regulation of the legitimate explosives industry and the elimination of the possession or use of explosives without a license or permit. Shortly thereafter, following a Treasury Department study of its func-

On September 11, 1794, the owners of most of the distilled spirits and stills operations signed an "oath of consent" to obey the new alcohol tax law, thus ending the rebellion against the whisky tariff.

tions, the division was removed from the Internal Revenue Service and given bureau status.

Keeping guns from criminal hands ranks as one of the most important missions of the Bureau of Alcohol, Tobacco and Firearms (ATF). During 1976 its agents seized more than 7,000 illegal firearms, including 900 submachine guns, sawed-off shotguns, and similar weapons. Agents made more than 3,000 arrests for gun violations. Among those arrested were 350 armed and dangerous "significant criminals," who were apprehended in a special program that involves the cooperation of ATF agents and state and local police in the enforcement of federal firearms laws.

ATF's National Firearms Tracing Center has helped solve many crimes involving the use of guns. While bureau agents originate many of the requests for assistance, slightly more than half of the center's traces are performed for state and local law enforcement agencies. The center traces a gun by contacting manufacturers, importers, wholesalers, and, eventually, the dealer who made the final sale. During 1976 more than fifty-one thousand traces were completed successfully, many of them leading to the solution of a serious crime.

To help its own and other federal agents and state and local law enforcement officers, the Bureau of Alcohol, Tobacco and Firearms maintains a firearms reference collection, a reference and research library that includes more than 2,500 different models of firearms. The collection is used to make comparison studies in preparing for court testimony, to determine if a firearm is designed chiefly for sporting, or other, purposes, to assist in the search for serial numbers, to help identify various brands and classes of guns, and to provide instruction in firearms identification.

In 1973 the Bureau of Alcohol, Tobacco and Firearms launched a two-year study that involved ten thousand guns seized by police in sixteen large United States cities. Results of the study indicated that guns used in street crimes are usually short-barreled and easily concealed. Moreover, one out of eighteen guns studied had been stolen. These and other findings of the bureau's Project Identification have been used in preparing anticrime legislation.

Investigative responsibilities in bombing incidents are shared by the Bureau of Alcohol, Tobacco

Wielding a sharp ax, an agent puts an illicit still out of business during Prohibition. In 1925 alone, Internal Revenue agents made 77,000 arrests and seized property valued at $11,200,000 while enforcing Prohibition laws.

Eliot Ness, the Treasury Department's most famous prohibition agent. Ness, whose exploits became famous through the novel The Untouchables *and a television series by the same name, headed an enforcement unit covering Illinois, Indiana, and Wisconsin.*

and Firearms, the Federal Bureau of Investigation, and the Postal Inspection Service. ATF investigates when one of its regulations is involved. It also investigates when a bombing involves property used in or affecting commerce, Treasury Department buildings or functions, or the interstate transportation of explosives with the intention of injuring individuals or destroying property. The FBI investigates bombings by terrorist or revolutionary groups and offenses against colleges and universities, United States property (other than Treasury or Postal), and foreign diplomatic facilities. The FBI also investigates bomb threats against individuals or property (other than Treasury or Postal). The Postal Inspection Service has jurisdiction when its facilities are involved. In cases where more than one agency appears to have jurisdiction, the Justice Department determines which one will conduct the investigation.

During 1975 and 1976, ATF agents investigated fifteen hundred explosive and incendiary bombings, one of them at the bureau's West Coast headquarters in San Francisco. In this field the bureau's efforts are directed primarily toward preventing the acquisition and use of explosives by criminals. For example, when 966 pounds of explosives were stolen in Toledo, Ohio, ATF agents quickly moved in and, working with local officers, arrested three persons and recovered most of the explosives before a sale could be arranged. In another case, agents were called in to investigate an explosion near Greenville, South Carolina, that destroyed a knitting mill. In the debris the agents found two unexploded sticks of dynamite, which were traced to a local construction firm. Although no theft of explosives had been detected by the firm, the agents located the employee who had stolen the dynamite. He, in turn, provided information that led to the conviction of two men, one of them the mill's owner, for conspiracy and for destroying the mill.

The Bureau of Alcohol, Tobacco and Firearms trains its own agents in the techniques of criminal bombing investigation and provides training for members of state and local law enforcement agencies.

Although traffic in illicit liquor has decreased, bureau agents continue to locate and seize moonshine distilleries, 557 in 1976, along with 11,000 gallons of liquor and 150,000 gallons of mash. Bureau arrests for liquor law violations totaled 460

Eliot Ness (behind wheel) *is pictured with two of his men.*

persons, of whom 90 percent pled guilty or were found guilty in the courts.

Regulations enforced by the Bureau of Alcohol, Tobacco and Firearms in 1976 affected 293 distilled spirits plants, wineries, breweries, 12,710 alcohol importers and wholesalers, 422,281 liquor and beer retailers, and 388 tobacco producers and warehousers. The $8 billion in alcohol and tobacco taxes collected by ATF was second only to personal and corporate income taxes as a source of revenue for the United States government.

Also under Bureau of Alcohol, Tobacco and Firearms regulation are some 160,000 firearms dealers, 780 firearms manufacturers and importers, and more than 6,700 ammunition makers. Licenses and permits issued to users, dealers, and manufacturers total more than five thousand.

Another Bureau of Alcohol, Tobacco and Firearms mission, which dates from December 1974, involved the enforcement of the federal wagering law that requires commercial gamblers to buy a special $500 tax stamp and pay a 2 percent excise tax on all bets that they book. In 1976 agents conducted 245 searches for illegal gambling activity, seizing more than a hundred automobiles and more than $234,000 in cash and securities. This function was transferred back to the Internal Revenue Service in 1977.

ATF maintains chemical, forensic, identification and test, and instrumentation laboratories in Washington and regional laboratories in Atlanta, Georgia; Cincinnati, Ohio; and Philadelphia, Pennsylvania. The laboratories perform technical and scientific studies for the bureau and offer their assistance without charge to state and local law enforcement agencies.

Scientists in ATF laboratories have developed advanced analytical techniques for use in explosives investigations. The laboratories also offer a wide range of document verification services, such as handwriting and typewriting identification, watermark examination, and the deciphering of obliterated writing.

The objective of all Bureau of Alcohol, Tobacco and Firearms programs is to ensure compliance with the laws it administers. Its criminal enforcement agents seek to eliminate illegal possession and use of firearms and explosives and to suppress traffic in illicit distilled spirits. The collection of revenue due from the alcohol and tobacco industries is the responsibility of the bureau's regulatory enforcement agents. The latter also investigate cases of commercial bribery, consumer deception, and other improper practices in the liquor industry.

A truckload of moonshine, after confiscation by Prohibition agents.

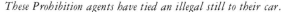

ATF's director, who is appointed by the secretary of the treasury, supervises the activities of the bureau from his headquarters in Washington. Because the bureau is decentralized, its approximately four thousand employees are stationed throughout the United States, working out of regional headquarters in Cincinnati, Philadelphia, Chicago, New York, Atlanta, Dallas, and San Francisco as well as the Washington headquarters.

These Prohibition agents have tied an illegal still to their car.

Most bombing investigations involve an exhaustive search of debris by Bureau of Alcohol, Tobacco and Firearms agents.

A serologist examines a blood sample in the ATF Forensic Laboratory.

Dusting evidence for fingerprints at ATF's Identification and Test Laboratory.

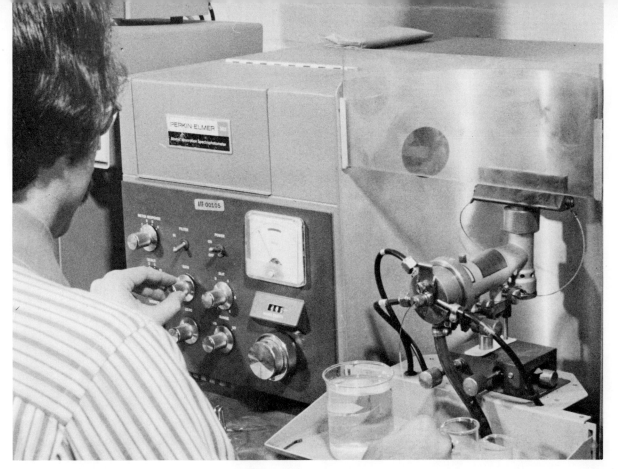

At the Bureau of Alcohol, Tobacco and Firearms Forensic Laboratory in Washington a scientist operates an atomic absorption spectrometer that determines the concentration of a particular element in a sample by measuring the amount of light absorbed by that element.

A Forensic Laboratory scientist uses a neutron activation system to determine the amounts of specific chemical elements in a sample.

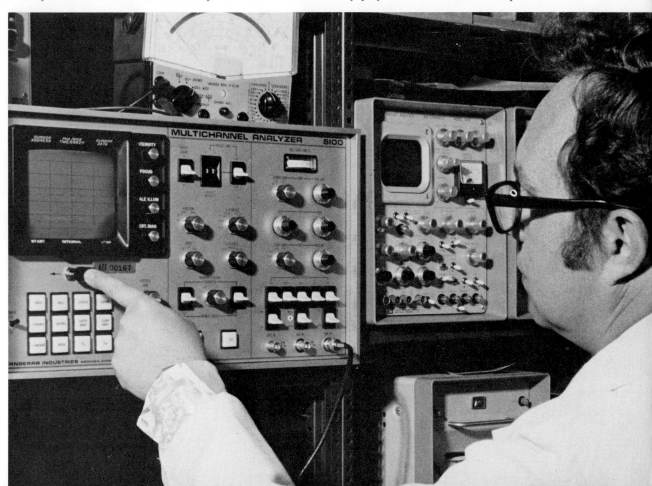

One of ATF's document examiners is comparing a suspicious signature on a certificate transferring ownership of a firearm with signatures that are known to be authentic.

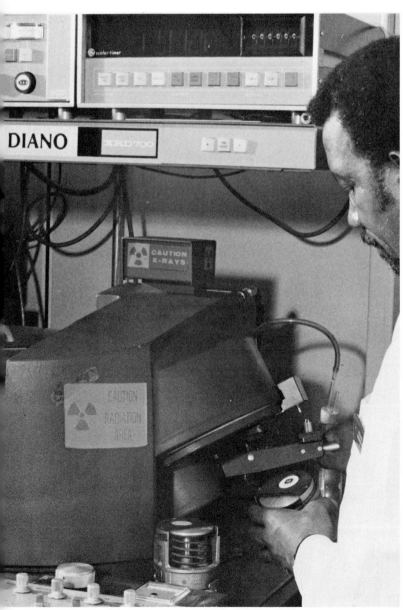

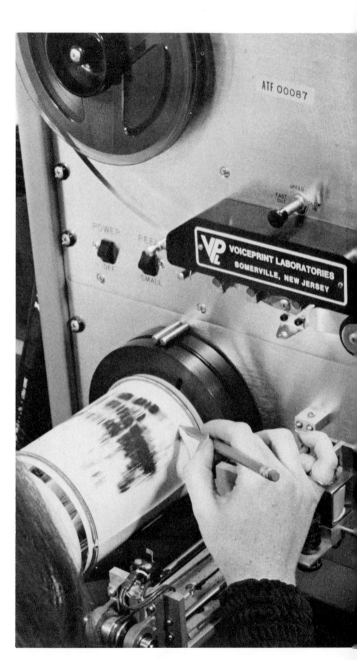

In ATF's Identification and Test Laboratory a speech pathologist is analyzing a voiceprint. Voiceprints aid in identification by revealing unique speech characteristics.

This Forensic Laboratory chemist is working with an X-ray diffraction analyzer. It will identify the crystal structure of the sample he is about to put into the analyzer.

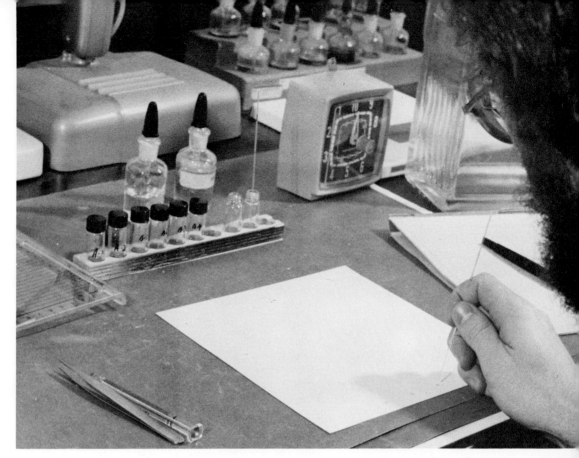

An ink chemist analyzes an ink. By comparing his results with the components of standard inks, he may be able to determine the manfacturer, date of first production, and formula number of the ink in question—information that he will pass on to ATF investigators.

The lines on the chart result from the breaking down of a sample into its components by a gas chromotograph, which then graphically displays the sample's composite nature. By comparing the chart with those of known products, the ATF scientist hopes to identify the sample.

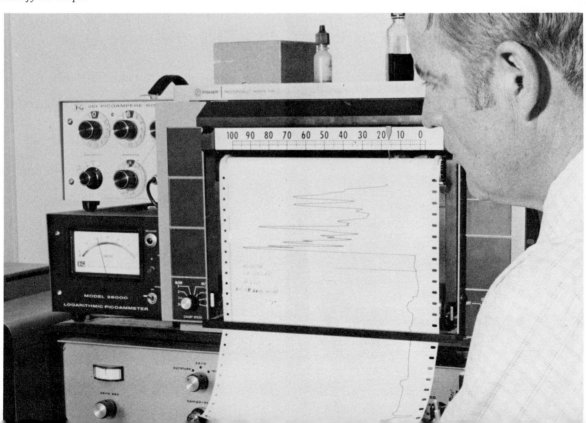

Bureau of Alcohol, Tobacco and Firearms agents shape up during training at the Federal Law Enforcement Training Center at Glynco, Georgia. In addition to the general training that all Treasury agents receive at Glynco, ATF trainees receive special instruction in the laws enforced by the bureau and the enforcement techniques that it uses.

This ATF Trainee is demonstrating his agility on the exercise field at Glynco.

Six of the standard strip stamps that alcohol bottlers purchase from the Bureau of Alcohol, Tobacco and Firearms as a tax and place over the mouths of their bottles to show that the contents have not been adulterated after leaving the distillery. Red stamps are used for ordinary domestically distilled spirits, green for spirits bottled in bond (the spirits must be at least four years old and 100 proof), blue for spirits bottled in bond for export, and white for industrial alcohol.

Scenes of anxious depositors lined up outside a bank were common in the early 1930s. Between 1930 and 1933 some nine thousand banks suspended operations.

Supervising the National Banks: The Office of the Comptroller of the Currency

ALTHOUGH THE OFFICE OF THE COMPTROLLER OF the Currency is a bureau within the Treasury, it operates almost separately from that department. Moreover, its name, descriptive when the agency was founded in 1863, no longer has meaning. Today, the relationship of the comptroller of the currency to United States currency is an indirect one arising from the comptroller's supervision of the country's national banks. The Office of the Comptroller considers applications for bank charters, approving or rejecting them after detailed and lengthy investigation. It grants permits for the formation of new branches of existing banks. It exercises broad administrative controls over bank mergers and consolidations. And it, among other duties, periodically examines approximately 4,700 chartered commercial banks, which hold about 60 percent of all United States bank deposits.

Commercial bank regulation by the federal government had its inception with the passage of the National Currency Act of 1863. The act established within the Treasury an agency called the Currency Bureau with a chief officer, the comptroller of the currency, appointed by the president with the advice and consent of the Senate. The comptroller was to conduct the affairs of the Currency Bureau under the general supervision of the secretary of the treasury, but Congress requested an annual report on all business transacted.

Because the comptroller of the currency was chiefly concerned with controlling the issue of national bank notes, an experienced banker seemed the obvious choice for that office. After two potential nominees declined, an Indiana banker, Hugh McCulloch, agreed to come to Washington, as he put it, "to organize the National Currency Bureau, with the understanding, however, that I should remain in Washington no longer than might be necessary to give the new banking system a successful start." McCulloch remained in office for two years. When he resigned in 1865 to become secretary of the treasury, Congress had passed a national bank act, and a national banking system was beginning to take shape.

Banks had not been established in colonial America largely because of the opposition of British merchants, who made a good thing of financing their American counterparts. The colonists also lacked experience with financial institutions.

The first American bank, the Bank of Pennsylvania, authorized in 1781 by the Continental Congress, was located in Philadelphia, then the financial center of the nation. It was replaced in 1784 by a successor institution, the Bank of North America, which for a time held charters issued by both federal and state authorities. Two other banks were chartered in 1784, the Bank of New York and the Massachusetts Bank, in Boston. Until 1790, these were the only commercial banks in the country. In that year the Bank of Maryland, in Baltimore, was added to a list that grew steadily until 1811, when there were eighty-eight banks.

Banks established in these early years were "founded on specie," that is, their capital was largely subscribed in gold and silver, and it was fully intended that both depositors and note holders would be able to obtain hard money on demand. Bank notes were ordered by the banks from private engravers whose numerous designs could be modified according to the whims of a particular board of directors. The notes were ordinarily signed by a bank's president and cashier and stored in the safe or vault until they were issued by a bank officer in the routine course of business.

During the first decades of our national history commercial banks were scrupulously run, their managements so conservative that many a creditworthy borrower was turned away empty-handed, although the more aggressive big-city bankers committed their institutions to the bonds of railroads and manufacturing companies as well as to those of states and municipalities. And gradually banks in the East began to engage in what was later called investment banking, the underwriting of securities issues. Banking practices tended to be less conservative, however, as banks were formed on the frontier.

Even in well-settled parts of the country, notes issued by different banks were accepted at widely varying rates. Notes of institutions long established and known to redeem in specie were accepted at par over wide areas. Bills of other banks were received at discounts varying from one-half of 1 percent to 50 percent or more. As much as anything else, distance from the location of the issuing bank affected the acceptability of notes. For example, notes of Baltimore banks might circulate at a 1 to 2 percent discount in Washington, forty miles away, with Washington paper discounted at 1 to 2 percent in Baltimore. The problem was particularly acute in the case of notes issued by banks in the West, which circulated in the East only at a big discount, even though they were

This portrait of Hugh McCulloch, the first comptroller of the currency, hangs in the office of the present comptroller.

issued by specie-paying banks with solid local reputations. Thus, the simplest transaction often involved haggling over the amount of payment required in the notes of a particular bank.

As the number of state banks increased to more than five hundred in 1834, the process of determining the value of the many kinds of genuine notes in circulation became more tedious and complex. To this difficulty was added the problem of detecting the growing number of counterfeit bills. Finally, there was the requirement that notes of closed banks, which often remained in circulation for long periods, be identified.

From the first days of the republic there had been advocates of federal regulation as the only way to en-

sure a widely accepted currency. Moreover, they insisted, only a bank with special powers could control the total money supply. Yet, there was great reluctance to give so much authority to the federal government, especially on the part of state-chartered banks whose officers and stockholders were persuaded that banking was more profitable in the absence of federally chartered institutions.

Soon after he became secretary of the treasury, Alexander Hamilton proposed the establishment of a bank of the United States. In his "Report on a National Bank," he argued that the young country required a major institution to provide a first-rate convertible paper currency and to serve as lender to the Treasury and fiscal agent for the government. Over the opposition of such noted statesmen as Thomas Jefferson and Edmund Randolph, Congress in 1791 followed Hamilton's advice and created the first Bank of the United States.

With a capital of $10 million, one-fifth of it subscribed by the government as a major stockholder, the Bank of the United States quickly became the most influential financial institution in the country. Following the clear intent of its charter, the bank earned most of its income by carrying on a regular commercial banking business that included maintaining checking accounts for its customers, financing credit needs, issuing bank notes, and transferring funds. The bank also made loans to the government and acted as its fiscal agent.

As Hamilton had predicted, the Bank of the United States provided valuable services to the government, including one that had not been foreseen, namely its regulation of loans by state banks whose notes entered circulation as money after being lent to borrowers. The rapid growth of the country and its economy had created a powerful demand for bank loans, and there was a constant danger of an overextension of credit that could lead to inflation and an economic crisis. Fortunately, the bank was able to exert a restraining influence. As a government depository with offices in the chief seaports and commercial centers, the bank received considerable sums in state bank notes from collectors of the customs and others doing business with the government. By redeeming these notes in gold or silver from the issuing institutions, the bank restricted the amount of collateral available for additional loans. On the other

hand, if business appeared to be slowing down, the bank could ease up on redemptions.

For its own loans the bank followed a conservative lending policy and, on balance, remained the creditor of the state banks, continually receiving a greater dollar volume of state bank notes than the state banks received of the bank's obligations. Notes of the Bank of the United States and its branches ordinarily circulated at par. The bank gradually came to hold a substantial portion of the country's monetary gold and silver, its vaults during the last three years of its existence containing about as much specie as the total holdings of the state banks. Moreover, the bank gradually took on the responsibility of making specie loans to state banks, many of which came to rely on the federal institution for accommodation in times of stress.

Senator John Sherman of Ohio, who introduced the Currency Act of 1863 establishing the Office of the Comptroller of the Currency. In 1877 Sherman became secretary of the treasury in President Rutherford Hayes's Cabinet.

The first Bank of the United States as it appeared in an engraving made in 1799. The bank was located in Philadelphia.

On January 7, 1817, after the first Bank of the United States had been closed for six years, a second Bank of the United States (seen here in a contemporary engraving) opened its doors. It was also located in Philadelphia.

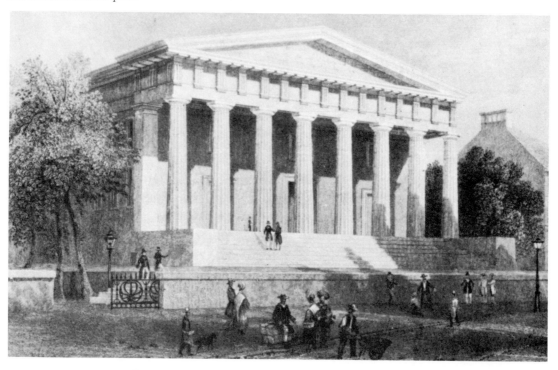

Some of the notes issued by Philadelphia's Bank of North America.

This $10 note was issued in 1824 by the Suffolk Bank of Boston.

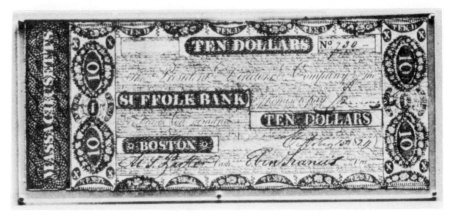

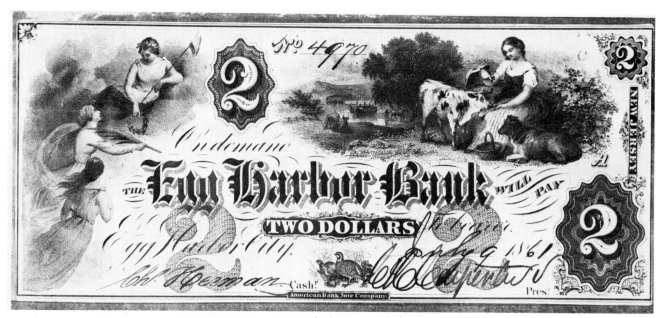

The Egg Harbor Bank, chartered by the state of New Jersey, issued this $2 note in 1861.

An early national bank note issued by the Third National Bank of Pittsburgh in 1865. The reverse (below) shows Sir Walter Raleigh exhibiting corn and smoking tobacco imported from America.

By almost any criterion, the first Bank of the United States was a success. Nevertheless, in 1811, a combination of opposition from agrarian and state banking interests, from critics who claimed that the bank was an instrument of the Federalist party, and from others who questioned its constitutionality led to the congressional rejection, by a narrow margin, of a bill to recharter the bank.

Grave financial problems arising from the War of 1812 and the deterioration of the paper currency issued by state banks led to renewed support for a federal banking institution. After congressional wrangling over several bills, the second Bank of the United States received its charter in 1816. With a capital of $35 million, one-fifth of it again subscribed by the government, the second bank soon became a major force in the economy. Like its predecessor, it acted as a central bank, controlling the quantity of money in circulation and rendering services to the federal government as well as to commercial banks. Its notes and those of its branches were literally as good as gold, circulating without discount throughout the United States. Branches of the bank provided banking facilities in backwoods areas and greatly reduced the cost to the business community of transferring funds from one part of the country to another.

Once again, agrarian conviction that the bank unduly restricted the money supply plus the hostility of state bankers, especially in New York and Boston, produced opposition to the bank's recharter. The bank became an issue in the election of 1832, and Andrew Jackson's victory was considered a defeat for pro-bank forces. A year later the government discountinued making deposits in the bank and, for all practical purposes, the United States again relinquished its central bank.

Both the first and second banks of the United States were required by their charters to furnish reports when called for by the secretary of the treasury, but not more often than once a week. These reports were to include the amount of capital stock issued, obligations due the bank, total deposits, and total notes on hand and in circulation. The secretary did not make the reports public, nor did he make them available to Congress unless some member asked for specific information. The secretary could, however, examine the books of the first and second banks, and the books of the second bank were also open to a congressional committee for examination.

Federal attempts to examine the condition of state banks developed purely by chance. In 1819 the House of Representatives, concerned over the administration of the second bank, passed a resolution demanding an inquiry into its activities and those of state banks as well. All state banks and banks in the District of Columbia were required to send the secretary of the treasury a statement showing their capitalization, notes issued and in circulation, public and private deposits, loans outstanding, and the value of specie in their vaults. In 1832 the House passed a resolution requiring the secretary to compile annually a report to Congress on the condition of the state banks, the data to be obtained from records of the governors or the legislatures of the states. These reports were submitted regularly, although with huge gaps in information, for thirty years.

Reports on the condition of the nation's banks did nothing to alleviate the problems inherent in a system in which the individual states chartered the banks. By 1860, for example, the more than fifteen hundred state banks had outstanding, on an average, six denominations of notes each; as many as nine thousand different kinds of paper bills were in circulation. Some were as good as gold; others passed at varying discounts. Notes of failed and voluntarily liquidated banks circulated long after the doors of the issuing institutions had closed forever. And with such a variety of designs to choose from, counterfeiters practiced a profitable trade.

On the whole, the pre–Civil War banking system worked well enough to encourage a rapid development of the economy that would have been impossible without the state banks. Nevertheless, the desperate financial situation in which the federal government found itself upon the outbreak of the Civil War required the action from Congress that resulted in the Currency Act of 1863, the National Bank Act of 1864, and the establishment of a national banking system.

After more than thirty years of remaining aloof, the federal government was again entering into a relationship with banks and bankers. Under the Currency Act, five or more people could form an "association" to establish a national bank, provided they could raise a capital stock of $50,000 in cities of ten thousand or less and $100,000 in cities of over ten thousand. Each association was required to deliver to the treasurer of the United States interest-bearing government bonds in an amount equal to one-third of the association's paid-in capital. If they wished, the associations could deposit bonds to the full amount of paid-in capital as security against their note issues, which could not exceed 90 percent of the market value of the United States bonds on deposit. The comptroller of the currency, as head officer of the Currency Bureau, was empowered to issue uniformly engraved notes to the associations. The total amount of such issues, not to exceed $300 million, was to be apportioned among the states in accordance with a formula that gave equal weight to population and to existing banking capital, resources, and business.

Because it was the administrative apparatus for the control of national bank note issues, Congress placed considerable importance on the Office of the Comptroller of the Currency. Presidential removal of a comptroller before the expiration of his five-year term required Senate advice and consent. Moreover, the comptroller's annual report was to be sent directly to Congress, bypassing the secretary of the treasury.

In spite of the urgent need to recruit member banks for the new national bank system, Hugh McCulloch, the first comptroller of the currency, opposed the automatic approval of charter applications. And before sending out forms to an applicant, he required information on the economic potential of the community in which the bank would be located, on the character and business ability of the bank's organizers, and on the banking facilities already available in the area of the proposed bank.

Comptroller McCulloch issued the first organizational certificate to the First National Bank of Philadelphia in June 1863. On November 28, 1863, he reported that 134 national banks had been organized, 94 of them in four states—New York, Pennsylvania, Indiana, and Ohio. Only one of the 134 banks represented a conversion of a state bank charter. The first of the new national bank notes began to circulate in December.

Comptroller McCulloch played an active role in the revision of the Currency Act of 1863 that resulted in the enactment of the National Bank Act of 1864. The Treasury Department has preserved the notebook in which he pasted sections of the 1863 act and penned lengthy proposals for amendments. Most of McCulloch's suggestions were incorporated in the 1864 act, which tightened and strengthened the original legislation.

In spite of the prestige of a national charter, most state banks preferred to remain with the more comfortable supervision they received under state charters. To encourage more banks to make the switch, Secretary of the Treasury Chase and Comptroller McCulloch recommended a high federal tax on state bank notes. In 1865 Congress imposed a 10 percent tax on the notes, and a year later only 297 state-

---

INSTRUCTIONS AND SUGGESTIONS
OF THE
COMPTROLLER OF THE CURRENCY
IN
REGARD TO THE ORGANIZATION AND MANAGEMENT OF NATIONAL BANKS.

TREASURY DEPARTMENT,
Office of the Comptroller of the Currency, 1864.

For the instruction and guidance of persons who may desire to organize National Banks, under the national currency act, the following suggestions and forms have been prepared:

1. In proceeding to organize an Association, the first thing to be done is to obtain the necessary subscriptions of stock. This may be accomplished through commissioners to be appointed for that purpose, or in any other manner that may be found to be the most convenient. No form is required by the Act, and it is not thought necessary that any should be furnished by this bureau. It is only necessary that the subscriptions should be made in such manner as will create a legal liability on the part of the subscribers to take and pay for the stock subscribed for by them respectively according to the requirements of the Act.

2. After the stock is taken, the associates should enter into Articles of Association, according to the requirements of the 5th section of the Act; and the following is submitted as a general form for such articles, to be modified in such proper manner as will meet the views of the persons forming Associations:

Page 1 of the Manual of Instructions *that Comptroller McCulloch sent to prospective organizers of national banks. First published in 1864, the manual remained in use, with revisions, for more than fifty years.*

chartered banks remained of the 1,089 that had existed in 1864. The number of national banks increased from 467 to 1,634 between 1864 and 1866. After 1875, however, the tax on their notes ceased to be an economic deterrent for the state banks.

Since there could be no truly national banking system without the conversion of the state banks, McCulloch and his immediate successors continued to work toward that end, giving preference in granting charters to state banks over new associations. This resulted in a disproportionate number of Eastern banks entering the system and an uneven distribution of national bank notes, with southern and western states complaining that they were not receiving their fair share. By 1875, however, charter applications from state banks no longer had preference, and Comptroller of the Currency John J. Knox was able to report: "Every application which has conformed to the requirements of the law has been granted."

With this letter, an Ohio bank examiner enclosed a list of the banks he had examined in August 1865, to earn the $475 due him.

During Knox's twelve-year tenure as comptroller of the currency, the granting of national bank charters became almost automatic if all requirements had been met, and most of the comptrollers who followed Knox in office agreed with his more lenient policies. Nevertheless, there was a resurgence of interest in state-chartered banking that resulted in the development of a dual banking system. Between 1880 and 1900 the number of national banks increased from 2,076 to 3,731. However, the number of state-chartered banks increased from 650 to just over 5,000 during the same period, reflecting in part the more lenient rules and examination procedures of the states.

Although the enforcement powers of the comptroller of the currency were not spelled out in detail, the records of national banks were subject to regular examination. For a continued infraction, the comptroller could revoke the charter of a national bank. For lesser violations, he relied on the cooperation of bank officers.

Comptroller McCulloch looked upon regular examinations as a means of exposing and checking "improper practices on the part of bankers, and violations of the wholesome provisions of the law." He sent a series of instructions to each of his examiners, instructions which he thought were necessary, but he pointed out that he could not issue what he called "cast-iron rules, covering minute details" to his examiners.

In Comptroller Knox's view, it was the "duty of the examiner to ascertain whether the officers of the bank and its directors are complying with the requirements of the law and whether they are in any way violating any of its provisions, to the end that in such case they may be enforced by proper authority." Knox went on to note that although the detection of embezzlement might occur as an incident of an examination expenses have been borne by the banks. of the examination. "It is scarcely to be expected," he wrote, "if a robber or a forger is placed in control of all its assets, that a national bank can be saved from disaster by the occasional visits of an examiner."

From the beginning of the national bank system, examination expenses have been borne by the banks. Some early bank examiners found this method of payment not to their liking. In 1864 one of Comptroller McCulloch's examiners wrote to him complaining of "considerable carriage fare, and Philadelphia expenses" and requesting $350. A New England examiner wrote that he had received no pay for examining sixty-one banks and asked the comptroller to tell him how much he was entitled to.

Legislation passed by Congress in 1875 established a system whereby most bank examiners received compensation based on the capital of each bank they examined. The remainder were to have their compensation fixed by the secretary of the treasury upon the recommendation of the comptroller of the currency. The banks continued to bear the cost of the examinations.

From their fees, examiners had to pay the wages of assistants and travel costs, hence it was to an examiner's advantage to hurry his work and get on to the next bank by the shortest possible route. Knowing this, bankers often were able to make fairly accurate guesses as to the approximate date of an examination and make preparations accordingly.

Over the years comptrollers requested higher pay for their examiners and the replacement of fees by a fixed salary, with an allowance for travel and other expenses. In 1893 Comptroller James H. Eckels noted in his *Annual Report*: "With a fixed salary instead of an already determined fee, examiners would be in a position to apportion their time, in making examinations, in accordance with the needs of the banks examined. Only in this way can be had that complete scrutiny of a bank's affairs which is due to the officers and shareholders and to its patrons and the general public."

In 1914 Congress finally abolished the fee system, replacing it with fixed salaries. The legislation also provided that examination costs were to be assessed against the banks in proportion to each bank's resources.

In addition to reports from his examiners, a comptroller received quarterly and monthly reports from the banks under his supervision. From time to time

John Knox, whose portrait appears on a national bank note series issued in 1902, was Comptroller of the Currency from 1872 until 1884.

James J. Saxon was comptroller of the currency from 1961 until 1966, a period during which national bank chartering and regulation policies were liberalized.

COMPTROLLER OF THE CURRENCY
FORM 1985
REV. FEB., 1965

APPLICATION TO ORGANIZE
A NATIONAL BANK AND
REPRESENTATIONS OF APPLICANTS

dated

_____ , 19 _____

THE COMPTROLLER OF THE CURRENCY
Washington, District of Columbia

APPLICATION

WE, THE UNDERSIGNED, intending to organize and operate a national bank in accordance with the provisions of the National Bank Act, as amended, do hereby make application to the Comptroller of the Currency for permission to organize said national bank, and propose as follows:

1. That the main office of said national bank be located at _____

_____ , in the _____ of _____ , County

of _____ , State of _____

2. That, in order of preference, said national bank have one of the following titles:

_____

_____

_____

Prospective national bank organizers must formally apply for a charter and undergo close personal and financial investigation by the Office of the Comptroller.

Two pages of the Report of Examination—the comptroller of the currency's bank examiners issue a detailed report of their findings.

A national bank charter certificate.

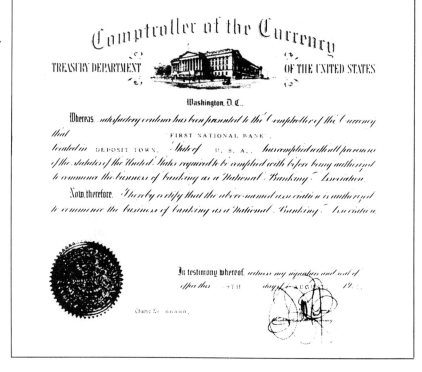

comptrollers expressed dissatisfaction with the quality of these reports. In 1867 Comptroller Hiland R. Hulburd complained: "It is known, understood, and anticipated, by all who have dealings with the banks, that they are in the habit of preparing systematically for making creditable exhibits on quarter day. It is certainly a point gained to know that the banks can make a good showing at least once every quarter; but it would be more satisfactory to know that they do so at all times."

Bank reports became more reliable after 1869 when Congress passed a law that allowed a comptroller to call for reports at random dates and for special reports as well, with penalties for noncompliance.

Toward the end of the nineteenth century the question of whether or not national banks should be allowed to open branches became an issue, with several comptrollers of the currency coming out in favor of branches, especially in rural areas where banking facilities were limited. One advocate of branches for national banks, Comptroller William B. Ridgely, stated in 1902: "I believe in branch banking. Theoretically it is the best system, as it is more economical, more efficient, will serve its customers better, and the organization can be such as to secure, in most respects, better management."

However, the National Bank Act of 1864 did not authorize branches, and by 1915 only twelve national banks maintained them. These were former state banks with branches that had converted to national charters. In spite of the urging of several comptrollers, it was 1933 before Congress passed a law setting up basic rules for the establishment of national bank branches.

While comptrollers, bankers, and congressmen were debating the pros and cons of branch banking, the panic of 1907–1908 had produced a rash of bank failures. The Office of the Comptroller responded to the crisis by scrutinizing charter applications more closely. At the same time, national bank supervision, in the beginning confined to ensuring that a bank could redeem its notes, became more exacting, a trend that accelerated with the inauguration of the Federal Reserve System in 1914. All national banks were required to enter the Federal Reserve System and to be examined by the comptroller of the currency at least twice a year. A national bank was also subject to examination by the Federal Reserve Board and by the Federal Reserve Bank of its district, a situation that led to strained relations between the comptroller of the currency and Federal Reserve officials. Several attempts to abolish the Office of the Comptroller of the Currency failed before tensions eased somewhat during the bank failure crisis of the early 1930s when the comptroller and the Federal Reserve Board worked together to rescue failing banks.

The Office of the Comptroller continues to share national bank supervision with the Federal Reserve Board, the latter also supervising state banks that are members of the Federal Reserve System. A third agency, the Federal Deposit Insurance Corporation, regulates the federally insured banks that are not members of the Federal Reserve System.

National banks, however, remain the responsibility of the comptroller of the currency who must see to it that laws and regulations relating to federally chartered banks are carried out. He makes sure that the 4,700 national banks and their 14,000 branches are soundly operated and are meeting the country's needs for commercial banking and trust services. Members of the comptroller's staff of two thousand examiners visit each national bank at least three times every two years and report the results of their examinations to the comptroller. In addition, the banks are required to publish financial statements four times a year.

In carrying out his regulatory responsibilities, the comptroller of the currency is assisted by several deputy comptrollers and a chief national bank examiner. Fourteen regional administrators supervise the activities of the bank examiners.

Unlike most federal agencies, the Office of the Comptroller of the Currency receives no government funds for its operations. Instead, it levies fees and assessments against the banks it regulates.

The Child That Is Older Than Its Parent: The United States Customs Service

AT THE END OF THE REVOLUTIONARY WAR THE fledgling United States government owed $52 million, $12 million in foreign debts and $40 million in domestic obligations, including unpaid interest amounting to $13 million. In addition, the war debts of the individual states added up to another $29 million. In this desperate situation, Congress found itself helpless. Under the Articles of Confederation it could not tax individuals; its legislation applied only to the state governments; and the state legislatures were reluctant to contribute money to the federal treasury. Moreover, the states were bickering among themselves on revenue matters. New York, for example, taxed firewood shipped into that state from Connecticut and vegetables, chickens, and eggs from New Jersey. In retaliation, Connecticut merchants agreed to boycott New York's products, while New Jersey levied a tax on a lighthouse owned by the City of New York.

Interstate rivalry in tariff matters continued in spite of efforts by the debt-ridden federal government to persuade the states to give Congress the authority to collect duties on imported goods. Finan-

The flag of the United States Customs Service with its sixteen alternate stripes of red and white shares a staff with the Star-Spangled Banner at the Customs Service's headquarters at 1301 Constitution Avenue N.W. in Washington.

cial collapse was a real possibility when the delegates to the Constitutional Convention assembled in Philadelphia in 1787, and the statesmen were well aware of the impending crisis. It is no wonder then that, in the section of the new Constitution dealing with the powers of Congress, Article I read: "To lay and collect taxes, duties, imposts and excises, to pay the debts and provide for the common defense and general welfare of the United States; but all duties, imposts and excises shall be uniform throughout the United States."

Congress passed the first United States Tariff Act on July 4, 1789. On the last day of that month it created a Customs Service with fifty-nine Customs districts in eleven states. On August 3 President Washington sent to the Senate the nomination of fifty-nine collectors, thirty-three surveyors, and ten naval officers for the Customs Service. With the exception of the naming of a charge d'affaires to the court of France, the Customs officers were the first presidential appointments under the new Constitution. Several of the appointees were Revolutionary War heroes, among them Generals Benjamin Lincoln, Sharp Delaney, Otho Williams, and John Lamb.

The Customs Service had been in existence for a month before Congress established the Department of the Treasury and gave it jurisdiction over customs matters, hence the description of the service as "the child that is older than its parent."

For many years Customs collectors' salaries came from specific fees and from a commission on the monies turned over to the Treasury. The salaries of the Customs Service's naval officers were based on half the fees collected. Surveyors, measurers, weighers, and gaugers were also paid from fees. Instructions received by Customs officers directed them to keep their accounts according to procedures established by the "proper department, or officers appointed by law to superintend the revenue of the United States."

In many American cities and towns Customs officers were the only representatives of the federal government other than judges and others connected with the judiciary. As a result, Customs employees performed various tasks in addition to the collection of duties. They gathered funds for the care of sick and disabled seamen and administered the Marine Hospital Service, now part of the U.S. Public Health Service. Collectors were in charge of lighthouses, and they enforced federal regulations governing coastal trade and the registry and clearing of vessels. The collectors also acted as pension agents for retired soldiers, and they gathered census information related to the nation's businesses and industries.

But the main function of the Customs Service was to collect revenue. Indeed, until the 1860s the duties collected by the service provided the federal government with its major source of income. The first vessel to arrive at a United States port after the Tariff Act of 1789 went into effect was the brigantine *Persis*, arriving from Italy. Customs agents assessed a duty of $774.71 on her cargo. During their initial year of operation, Customs agents collected approximately $2 million for the Treasury. In ensuing years Customs revenues paid for the Louisiana Purchase, the War of 1812, the Mexican War, the Gadsden Purchase, and the first two years of the Civil War.

Alexander Hamilton, George Washington's able secretary of the treasury, devoted a great deal of time to the operation of the Customs Service that provided most of his revenue. He personally wrote much of the legislation setting up machinery for the enforcement of tariff laws that Congress passed in 1790. One section of that legislation called for a fleet of "revenue cutters or boats," the forerunner of the

United States Coast Guard. Another section laid the foundation for a duty-free interstate transportation system by making it unlawful for Delaware to tax imported goods passing through that state between the ports of Baltimore and Philadelphia. The legislation was later extended to shipments of foreign goods between other cities.

Congress authorized a flag for the Customs Service in 1799. Originally the flag, which now flies at all ports of entry, was intended for use on vessels of the Revenue Cutter Service. Thirteen stars and an eagle holding an olive branch with thirteen leaves in one claw and thirteen arrows and a shield in the other decorate the union of the Customs flag. The remainder of the flag consists of sixteen alternate stripes of red and white, the stripes representing the sixteen states that made up the union in 1799.

Customs collectors were in the thick of events leading up to the War of 1812. They were called upon to enforce the Embargo Act of 1807, which Congress passed to cut off Great Britain's profitable trade with the United States. The suspension of trade with Canada the following year increased enforcement problems as smugglers and otherwise law-abiding citizens insisted upon their right to trade with whomever they wished. The ingenious methods used by smugglers and the multiplicity of locations where goods could be moved into or out of the country proved almost too much for the Customs Service. In 1808 the collector in Vermont complained to Secretary of the Treasury Albert Gallatin that he could not enforce the trade regulations without military assistance. Gallatin responded with permission for the collector to hire and equip crews and arm as many vessels as necessary to enforce the law. In some cases, however, soldiers were assigned to Customs Service vessels.

The war itself, with its stringent shipping regulations, severely taxed the resources of the Customs Service. Smuggling was extensive, with the British army often the beneficiary. Writing in 1814, the governor-general of Canada stated: "Two-thirds of the Army in Canada are at this moment eating beef provided by American contractors."

During its first century of existence, whether the United States was at war or enjoying peace, the organization of the Customs Service changed only slightly. Many Customs officials, especially the collectors, comptrollers, appraisers, and surveyors, were political appointees, as were numerous other government employees of the day. A change in the party in power meant a sweeping change in Customs personnel, with the new appointees often knowing little about the duties they were expected to perform. In addition, the payment of salaries and expenses from customs duties led to abuses. After 1849 all customs receipts were paid directly to the Treasury and Congress made an annual appropriation for the operation of the Customs Service.

It was not until the passage of the Civil Service Act in 1881 that selection for federal employment on the basis of merit began to replace the spoils system. However, Customs did not become an all-career service until 1965, when the position of collector of customs was abolished, a move that saved the government $1 million a year.

Now owned by the Daughters of the American Revolution and open to the public on occasion, the old customhouse at Yorktown, Virginia, is believed to be the first such edifice in the Thirteen Colonies. It was built in 1706 and served as a customhouse until 1845.

Philadelphia's marble Old Custom House, erected between 1819 and 1824, housed the second Bank of the United States before it became a customhouse. The building has been restored.

The Charleston Custom House, completed in 1879 and still standing.

Some Famous Nineteenth-Century Customhouses

The historic Boston Custom House in a photo taken prior to 1915. The custom house opened for business in 1838.

During the 1840s Nathaniel Hawthorne worked in this customhouse at Salem, Massachusetts. Built in 1819, it is now open to visitors as part of the Salem Maritime National Historic Site.

In 1915 a five-hundred-foot tower was added to the Boston Custom House giving it the appearance seen here. The building is still in use.

This nineteenth-century engraving shows disembarking passengers undergoing customs inspection at a New York City dock.

Customs underwent a major reorganization in 1912. Functions were realigned, unnecessary offices were closed, regulations were rewritten, and pay scales were revised. After World War I began in Europe in 1914, the reorganized Customs Service enforced United States neutrality laws at the country's ports and harbors, an assignment that involved inspecting suspicious cargoes, controlling the use of wireless apparatus by vessels in United States ports, and investigating attempts to damage shipping.

When the United States entered the war in 1917, the Customs Service took into custody seventy-nine enemy ships caught in United States ports. Customs officers licensed imports and exports, checked all shipments to and from the United States, and examined all passengers and baggage leaving the country. They also censored film, letters, and other communications passing through the ports. These added duties led to the organization of the Customs Intelligence Bureau with headquarters at the Port of New York, the center of the Customs Service's wartime activity. Because the volume of work there was

Conducting business in the San Francisco Custom House circa 1900.

so great, the Treasury Department authorized the hiring of three hundred temporary workers at $4 a day. Men who were exempt from the draft were urged to "do their patriotic duty" at the port and many more responded than could be hired. Outfitted in olive drab coats, trousers, overcoats, and caps, CIB men performed a variety of duties. They issued certificates of citizenship to American seamen, supervised the activities of vessels in port and the actions of their crews, and maintained a harbor patrol. The Customs Intelligence Bureau was disbanded when the war ended.

Scarcely had the Customs Service reverted to its peacetime function of collecting and protecting the revenue when Congress passed the Volstead Act outlawing the sale of alcoholic beverages. Illegal liquor became a big business. Some alcohol was manufactured in American stills, but much of it was smuggled into the country. Customs officers along the Canadian and Mexican borders as well as those

Officers assigned to the Black Rock Custom House in Buffalo, New York, posed for this group portrait in 1905. Although an 1884 regulation stated, "At ports where a uniform is required to be worn, it must be worn on regular duty," Customs Service uniforms were neither standardized nor required nationwide until the close of World War I.

stationed on the coasts tried to stop the flow, an effort that cost the lives of some forty Customs men before the 18th Amendment was repealed in 1933.

As a retired Customs officer, Fred W. Maguire remembered Prohibition-era smugglers as a clever lot. "They used to use every trick in the book to ship liquor into the country," he recalled. "They used boats with false decks that concealed countless gallons of liquor lashed down in the concealed areas.

"One bunch in Michigan had a real clever scheme going. They used a long, torpedolike metal cylinder, waterproofed it, filled it with liquor, and pulled it across a lake on the border by using a steel cable. They submerged the cylinder five feet below the surface and only used it at night. One of our men spotted the rig glistening on a clear moonlit night.

"Every trip brought fifteen more gallons into the country. By the time we arrested the men, they had thousands of gallons of bootleg liquor stored and awaiting sale."

Another Customs Service veteran of the Prohibition era was, like Maguire, a member of the Custom Service's mounted border patrol, a force that served on the Mexican and Canadian borders until 1948 when the patrol was disbanded. Of his fellow border

This photograph of Customs Intelligence Bureau members was taken in New York City's Battery Park during World War I. The Intelligence Bureau was organized along military lines into sections and squads or platoons.

patrol inspectors, J. F. Weadock wrote: "These were men who were called on to enforce Prohibition along a border so rough and isolated it would have taken a small army to do the job. Later, as other men joined forces with Customs, the mileage to be covered still made full enforcement a joke to the men on the line.

"It is to the everlasting credit of the service that few men who wore the Customs badge succumbed to the lure of easy money, which was offered them. In fact, when one man did succumb, he was soon detected by the men he worked with. His chief showed personal hurt when he had to turn the man over to the Justice Department."

From 1875 until 1927 the Customs Service, its usual designation, was one of the Treasury Department's divisions. In 1927 it became the Bureau of Customs under the direction of a commissioner appointed by the secretary of the treasury. (In 1973 the bureau officially became the United States Customs Service.) Whatever may have been the intention of Congress when it made the change from Treasury division to Treasury bureau, commissioners of customs exercised little real control over the agency. Instead,

the field staff managed the affairs of the forty-nine districts with a minimum of guidance from Washington. It was not until the 1940s that a commissioner of customs began to assume more authority over his field staff. That commissioner, W. R. Johnson, an appointee of Secretary Henry Morgenthau, Jr., later became the only commissioner of customs to be removed involuntarily from his post. His dismissal resulted from a dispute with Congress over the implementation of a budget cut.

Two members of the Customs Border Patrol on duty on the Arizona-Mexico border. When the patrol was formed in 1853, members were required to supply at their own expense two pistols, a rifle, a pony, and a pack mule. The patrol was disbanded in 1948.

The Southwest Border Patrol was holding a conference in El Campo, California, when this photograph was taken circa 1930.

The great increase in international trade and travel that followed World War II brought changes to the United States Customs Service. In 1956, for example, 129 million persons crossed the borders of the United States and customs collections totaled a record $983 million. Its growing volume of business forced the service to simplify its more complex procedures, some of which had been in the regulation books for a century and a half. After 1953, every calculation of customs duty no longer had to be verified by a service comptroller before it could be collected. Goods could be imported without a certification by

For some of their border patrols Customs Service inspectors used an automobile, which was replaced with a horse when the terrain became difficult. This photo was taken in the state of Washington's Northwest Patrol District sometime between the two world wars.

Winter patrols along the Canadian border required special equipment. Here are inspectors with snowshoes and an early form of the snowmobile in a photograph taken prior to 1947, when the Canadian border patrol was discontinued.

After joining the Custom Service's patrol force in 1974, these Papago Indians were assigned to their own reservation, which borders on Mexico.

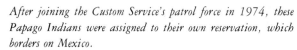

the United States consul in the country of origin. And clerical errors in duty computations were corrected without court action.

Travelers as well as commercial importers benefited from the easing of regulations. United States residents visiting Canada for less than forty-eight hours were allowed to bring back $10 worth of merchandise free of duty, an increase from the previous $1 limit. And duty-free purchases could be returned for repair or exchange without complicated customs procedures. Automobiles carrying tourists from Canada or Mexico no longer had to be registered at the border.

Other changes involved simplified baggage declaration forms and speeded-up customs examinations. There was also a new emphasis on courteous treatment for the traveler by Customs Service personnel. But ensuring the collection and protection of revenue due under the tariff regulations of the United States and the enforcement of customs and related laws remained the primary responsibilities of the Customs Service officer.

Among the laws that the United States Customs Service is called upon to enforce are those forbidding the importation into the United States of narcotic and dangerous drugs. The smuggling of drugs has always been a concern of the Customs Service. It was not until the problem reached epidemic proportions at the end of the 1960s, however, that the service received the funding that enabled it to become America's "first line of defense" in the war against illegal drugs. Although the major responsibility for the control of drugs was transferred in 1973 to a newly created agency, the Drug Enforcement Administration in the Department of Justice, the Customs Service, through its Office of Investigations, remains active in drug interdiction. During fiscal year 1976 the service's agents seized $667,889,544 worth of illegal drugs. Seizures were made both at and between ports of entry. In the latter case, the service had the use of a support system that included high performance aircraft, light spotter aircraft, helicopters, infrared sensors, airborne and mobile ground radar, and a sophisticated communications network.

The ingenuity of the drug smuggler poses a constant challenge to the Customs agent. Among many other hiding places, drugs have been discovered in

In 1947 Kathleen I. Dixon, a Customs Service inspector in Miami, Florida, became the first female customs officer to wear a uniform. After many years of being restricted to secretarial jobs, women have also moved into such formerly male-dominated Customs Service positions as special agent, import specialist, operations officer, and law specialist.

almost every part of the automobile, in stereo speakers, in gift packages supposedly containing food, in shoes, and on various parts of the smuggler's body.

In 1970 the discovery by Customs agents of ninety-three pounds of heroin in a light aircraft parked at Miami International Airport resulted in the arrest and conviction of Auguste Joseph Ricord, a major smuggler. Acting on a tip that French heroin was being flown into the United States by way of Paraguay and supplied with a list of aircraft that might be involved, agents searched the suspected craft. After finding heroin packed in three false-bottomed suitcases, they arrested the plane's pilot and copilot who implicated Ricord. Through the cooperation of the Paraguayan government, Ricord was arrested in that country and extradited to the United States where he was tried and convicted.

Dogs trained to detect drugs have helped Customs agents in their battle against drug smuggling, particularly in smuggling that involves mail parcels, cargo shipped into the United States, and vehicles driven or shipped across United States borders. During 1967, their first year on the job, detector dogs located more than $3 million worth of illegal drugs.

Although the apprehension of drug smugglers and the confiscation of illegal drugs receive widespread publicity, drugs are not the only commodities that smugglers try to bring into the United States. Customs agents keep a constant lookout for travelers who are transporting gold, diamonds, jewelry, watches, liquor, guns, art objects, and pornography that they have failed to declare. Commercial impor-

ters are also scrutinized for attempts to defraud the Treasury.

In addition to its enforcement of customs laws and regulations that produced $4,957,810,389 for the Treasury in fiscal year 1976, the Customs Service performs a number of functions for other government agencies that can best be accomplished when goods or travelers are entering the United States. Customs agents enforce regulations protecting wild animals and birds of the endangered species, plant and animal quarantine regulations, and safety regulations for imported vehicles and equipment. They also enforce the prohibition on the discharge of refuse and oil into or upon the coastal waters of the United States. In all, the United States Customs Service carries out regulatory or control activities for some forty different federal agencies, while it continues to collect and protect the revenue, a task that it successfully has discharged for almost two hundred years.

Here, an advanced management training course for Customs Service officials is in session. The service provides a variety of training programs for its personnel.

Customs agents apprehended this smuggler during the Prohibition era. Concealing contraband on the body remains a common method of smuggling and one of the easiest to detect.

Zeroing in on the Smuggler

Customs inspectors discovered hashish in these Nescafé jars.

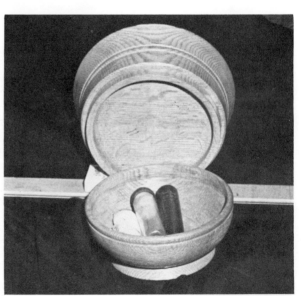

The lower portion of this double wooden bowl contained smuggled diamonds in the two plastic tubes. The third object is an ordinary spool of thread. The bowl was carried in the luggage of an airplane passenger.

The evidence in an ingenious smuggling scheme that failed. The wine bottle had been split horizontally into two sections just below the neck. After filling the lower part of the bottle with narcotics, the smugglers inserted a glass partition, rejoined the two halves, and poured wine into the upper section.

Customs Service officers examine 250 pounds of gold bullion discovered in the gas tank of an automobile, a hiding place frequently used by smugglers.

A Customs Service inspector removes one of twenty-two packages of marijuana found in the gas tank of a car being examined at the San Ysidro, California, customs port.

In New York a seaman was caught as he came ashore with marijuana hidden in his boots.

Customs inspectors are on the alert for the false bottoms in trunks, suitcases, and other containers that can be used to conceal smuggled goods, in this case, pearls.

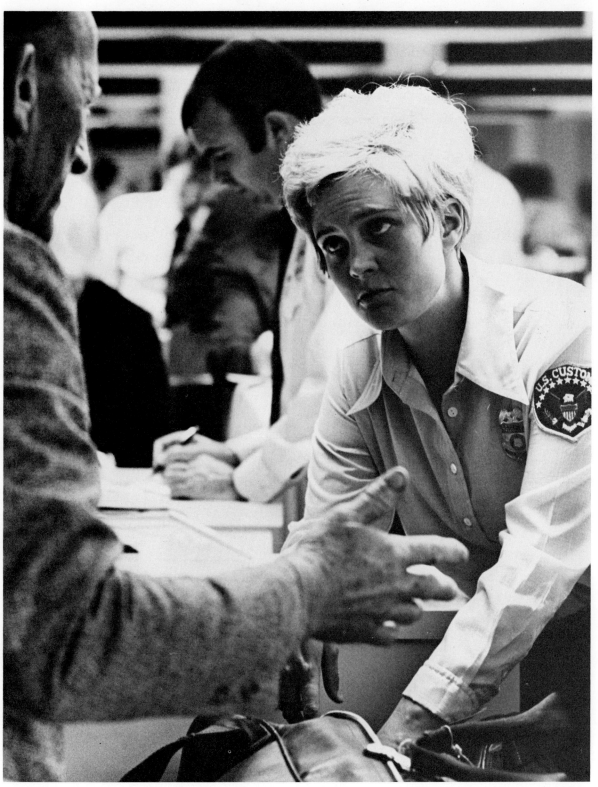

A Customs Service inspector examines the luggage of a passenger who has arrived in the United States on a flight that originated in another country.

These liquor bottles, seized at San Ysidro, California, were filled with the real thing. The liquor had not been declared, however, and exceeded the duty-free exemption of one quart per person.

One of the responsibilities of the Customs Service officer is to exclude from the United States insects and other pests that could bring disease to plant, animal, or human life. An inspector has found several mangoes hidden in an automobile. The mangoes could harbor undesirable insects. The Customs Service helps enforce some twenty laws related to the protection of the environment or the consumer.

This Customs Service patrol officer was photographed as he radioed a report on ship arrivals at New York.

In their search for contraband, Customs Service inspectors are assisted by dogs trained to sniff out marijuana and illegal drugs. For reasons of safety, dogs are not used to search people.

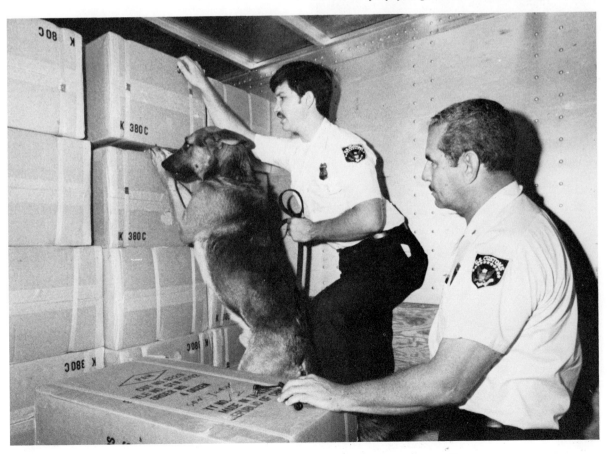

Customs Service agents are on hand to check the manifests of ships that unload cargo at United States ports. This photo was taken at the port of Baltimore.

In addition to collecting duties on automobiles imported into the United States, the Customs Service makes sure that they meet the safety and emission standards required by United States laws. This Mercedes-Benz will be examined by customs inspectors before it is released to the importer.

When a ship arrives in the United States from a foreign port, Customs Service officers have only a few hours to look for hidden contraband. An agent conducts a search in a ship's hold.

Much of the smuggled merchandise seized by the Customs Service is disposed of at annual auctions held in various parts of the country. Here an auction is under way in Washington, D.C.

A view of the warehouse at Los Angeles where imported merchandise is held pending examination and assessment of customs duties.

In this photo taken at Detroit's Harbor Terminal a Customs Service import control team checks incoming merchandise for false invoicing.

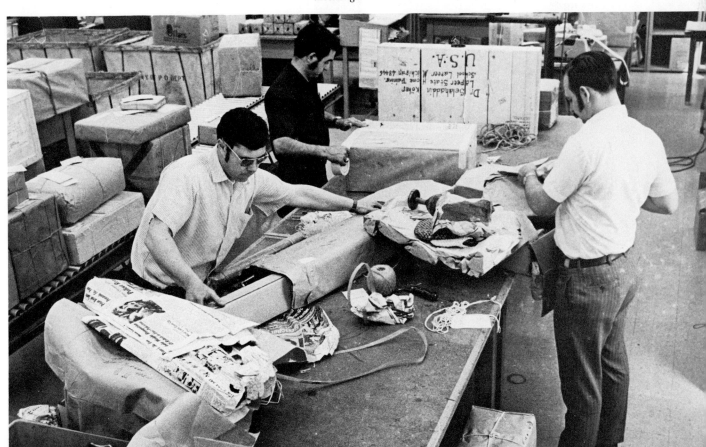

The Customs Service's general chemical laboratory in Savannah, Georgia, is one of eleven laboratories equipped to examine imports for evaluation purposes and to determine if they contain harmful ingredients.

These Custom Service chemists are checking the strength of imported dye.

An imported powder is under scrutiny.

When this photo was taken in a New Orleans laboratory, Customs Service chemists were analyzing samples of fluorspar, a mineral used in glassmaking.

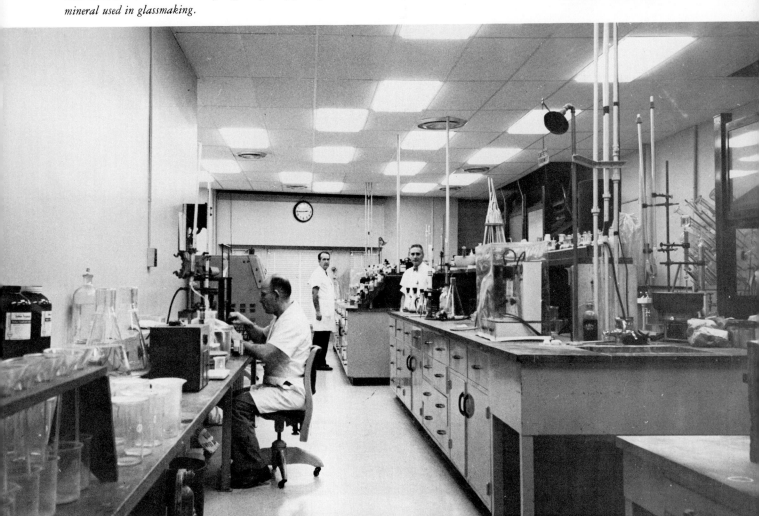

The Treasury's Navy: The United States Coast Guard

UNTIL 1967, THE DATE OF ITS TRANSFER TO THE Department of Transportation, the United States Coast Guard was a component of the Department of the Treasury. The relationship between the Treasury and the Coast Guard is an old one, dating back to 1790 when Secretary of the Treasury Alexander Hamilton asked Congress to appropriate funds to purchase a fleet of ten boats with which the secretary proposed to enforce the Tariff Act of 1789. Because the tariff legislation had failed to produce the expected revenue, Congress authorized Hamilton's boats, with the provision that the $10,000 needed for their purchase come out of customs duties.

The first of the Treasury's cutters to take to the seas was the *Massachusetts*, launched in 1791 and destined for duty off the coast of the state for which she was named. The nine remaining cutters soon joined the *Massachusetts* in guarding the coast against smugglers, an enterprise that received much attention from Secretary Hamilton. He recommended to the officers commanding the vessels that they make extensive patrols in the neighborhood of their stations. To remain in one place, he pointed out, would allow "fraudulent practices" everywhere else. Hamil-

A suspected submarine was the target when this photograph was taken on a Coast Guard-manned vessel during an Atlantic crossing.

ton was well aware that the Treasury lost badly needed revenue when tariff regulations were ignored. "It is now indispensable that they should be strictly enforced," he told his cutter masters who, as Customs Service officers, took an oath to support the Constitution and to prevent and detect frauds against the laws of the United States imposing duties upon imports.

Along with their function as Customs Service officers, the men of the Treasury's Revenue Cutter Service were called upon to defend their country upon the high seas. In fact, until Congress created a Navy Department in 1798, the revenue cutters were the nation's only naval combat force. After the formation of the navy, the cutters acted in cooperation with navy vessels to protect United States coasts and shipping during wartime. Nine cutters joined the navy's combat force when the United States declared war on Great Britain in 1812. Although the Treasury's vessels were small, they acquitted themselves well in combat, capturing fourteen enemy ships, most of them larger and more heavily armed.

In 1836 the men of the Revenue Service interrupted their pursuit of smugglers and the pirates operating along the eastern and southern coasts to cooperate with the navy and the army in a war with the Seminole Indians, who were resisting attempts to relocate them west of the Mississippi River. In 1846 the service, now in the process of converting to iron hulls and steam power for its vessels, sent nine cutters to Mexican waters when the United States declared war on that country. The cutters transported men and supplies, delivered messages and patrolled coastal waters looking for shipping bound for enemy ports.

During the Civil War, the Revenue Service having resumed its cooperation with the navy, Secretary of the Treasury Salmon P. Chase urged his cutter

The Coast Guard emblem, as revised in 1967.

captains to employ "utmost vigilance" as they sought to interdict shipments that could aid the Confederate cause. Cutter patrols stopped vessels bound for the Confederate states and acted to prevent goods, chiefly cotton, from leaving Confederate ports. The cutters also protected Union shipping and assisted Union military campaigns.

Following the purchase of Alaska in 1867 the Revenue Cutter Service extended its peacetime operations to that area. In some cases, as the only readily available representative of the United States government, it added legal and medical services to its more customary duties. Cuttermen also helped explore the vast new territory, delivered mail and supplies, transported government officials, and collected specimens of animal and plant life for the Smithsonian Institution. And in 1891 the cutter *Bear* sailed to Siberia where her crew purchased

Launched in 1791, the Massachusetts *was the first and the largest of the original ten revenue cutters. The vessel remained in service until 1798 when she was sold.*

twelve reindeer for shipment to Alaska, the first of more than a thousand reindeer brought to the territory by the Revenue Cutter Service to ensure a food supply for Eskimos whose traditional sources of food were disappearing.

On the other side of the continent, the Revenue Service was chosen to patrol the North Atlantic for the International Ice Patrol, formed after the sinking of the British liner *Titanic* following a collision with an iceberg. The ships and planes of the United States Coast Guard maintain that patrol today. Other lifesaving operations that involved the Treasury Department through its Revenue Cutter Service included the shore-based Lifesaving Service and the Lighthouse Service.

In 1915 the Revenue Cutter Service and the Lifesaving Service were combined to form the United States Coast Guard with 4,155 officers and men, 45 cutters of various types, and 280 lifeboat stations.

(The Lighthouse Service had been transferred to the Commerce and Labor Department in 1903.) Ellsworth P. Bertholf, the former head of the Revenue Cutter Service, became the captain commandant of the Coast Guard under the direction of the secretary of the treasury. The legislation that created the Coast Guard also provided that the new organization was to be a part of the military forces of the United States. During a war, or at the request of the President, the Coast Guard was to operate as part of the navy. Accordingly, the Coast Guard's cutters joined navy vessels during World War I, primarily to battle the German submarine fleet.

Its peacetime role as a Treasury agency charged with preventing smuggling involved the Coast Guard in the enforcement of the Prohibition amendment. The service's offshore patrols attempted to keep suspected ships under surveillance and to intercept illegal liquor shipments. During the fourteen

On March 21, 1791, President George Washington signed the commissions of the first thirteen officers appointed to serve on the ten revenue cutters then under construction. The certificate showing the commission of one of these men, Hopley Yeaton, is reproduced here. It is the only one of the thirteen still in existence.

GEORGE WASHINGTON, President of the United States of America.

TO ALL WHO SHALL SEE THESE PRESENTS, *GREETING.*

KNOW YE, That reposing special Trust and Confidence in the Integrity, Diligence and good Conduct of *Hopley Yeaton of New Hampshire* . . . . I DO APPOINT him *Master* . of a Cutter in the Service of the United States, for the Protection of the Revenue; and do authorize and empower him to execute and fulfil the Duties of that Office according to Law; AND TO HAVE AND TO HOLD the said office, with all the Rights and Emoluments thereunto legally appertaining, unto him the said *Hopley Yeaton* . . during the Pleasure of the President of the United States for the Time being.

IN TESTIMONY whereof I have caused these Letters to be made Patent, and the Seal of the United States to be hereunto affixed. GIVEN under my Hand, at the City of Philadelphia, the *Twenty first* . Day of *March* . in the Year of our Lord one thousand seven hundred and ninety *one* , and of the Independence of the United States of America the *Fifteenth.*

G Washington

By the President

Th Jefferson

Since 1799 the Coast Guard ensign in various forms has flown on United States vessels engaged in enforcing maritime law as a symbol of their authority. An emblem, added to the seventh red stripe in 1910, assumed the form shown here in 1927.

This painting by an unknown artist shows a Revenue Service cutter (right) confronting a large English brig during the War of 1812.

years that the 18th Amendment was in force, the Coast Guard seized thousands of vessels with their crews and cargoes.

Airplanes as well as ships were used by the Coast Guard in its war against the illegal importation of liquor, and aviation continued to play a part in Coast Guard enforcement and lifesaving activities. In 1937 Secretary of the Treasury Henry Morgenthau, Jr., reported that the Coast Guard had flown a total of almost 3 million miles during which its pilots had saved lives, detected smugglers, located obstructions to navigation, aided vessels in distress, and performed other valuable services.

For the Coast Guard World War II meant a return to operating as a part of the navy. Coastguardsmen performed antisubmarine and convoy escort duties, but perhaps their most significant contribution to the war effort was in amphibious landing operations. Throughout the war years the Coast Guard continued its missions for the Treasury Department, although on a somewhat limited scale.

After nearly 177 years in the Treasury Department the Coast Guard was transferred to the newly created Transportation Department in 1967. However, the Coast Guard continues to cooperate with the Treasury's Customs Service to prevent the illegal landing of dutiable goods and prohibited imports, such as dangerous drugs, and in other enforcement programs, including pollution control in United States coastal waters.

This illustration of the uniforms worn by United States Navy officers in 1830 was based on navy orders and contemporary engravings. Revenue Service officers probably wore similar uniforms.

During the Seminole War men of the Revenue Service transported soldiers and marines on Florida's many waterways.

The cutter Walter Forward *as she appeared shortly after the Mexican War. During that conflict she assisted in the capture of eleven enemy vessels. The* Forward *ended her government service in 1865 when she was sold.*

The yacht Henrietta, *shown here under sail, was purchased for Civil War blockade duty with the Revenue Cutter Service. For a time the yacht's former owner served aboard her as a first lieutenant.*

The cutter Lincoln, *shown here at anchor at Victoria, British Columbia, in 1870, carried the official party to Alaska for the formal taking-over ceremonies following the purchase of Alaska from Russia in 1867. After ten years of service with the cutter fleet, the* Lincoln *was sold in 1874.*

For many years Revenue Service and Coast Guard cutters transported a "Floating Court" to the remote areas of Alaska. Shown here is the court in session at Homer, Alaska, with Judge Joseph W. Kehoe (right) presiding.

Alvan A. Fengar, a newly appointed first lieutenant in the Revenue Cutter Service, posed for this photograph in 1862. Fengar later became the first Revenue Service skipper of the famous Arctic cutter Bear.

Natives (left) *watch as crewmen hoist a reindeer aboard the* Bear *in a picture taken on August 28, 1891. The* Bear *was getting ready to sail from Siberia with twelve domesticated deer purchased to introduce reindeer husbandry to Alaska.*

In 1913 the 190-foot cutter Miami (shown here) *and the cutter* Seneca *performed the first Ice Patrol for the Revenue Cutter Service.*

A rescue at sea. On Easter Sunday, 1914, the British freighter Columbian, *bound for New York, caught fire and blew up in the North Atlantic. One of its lifeboats, located by the cutter* Seneca *after it had been adrift for ten days, was photographed as the cutter drew alongside. Only four of the lifeboat's original fourteen passengers survived.*

The cutter Acushnet, *on International Ice Patrol in 1952, has located a large berg in the North Atlantic.*

Ellsworth P. Bertholf, the first captain commandant of the United States Coast Guard at his desk in Washington. Bertholf directed the Revenue Cutter Service from 1911 until 1915 and the Coast Guard from its formation in 1915 until 1919.

The cutter Tampa *as she appeared at the outbreak of World War I. As the* Miami, *the name she bore until 1916, she served as the first Ice Patrol for the Revenue Cutter Service. In 1918, while on duty with the Atlantic Fleet Patrol Forces, the* Tampa *sank with the loss of 131 lives, the probable victim of a German submarine.*

A U.S. Life-Saving Service crew is bringing five persons ashore from a shipwreck. Between 1871 and 1941 there were 203,609 such rescues.

Coastguardsmen from a rescue station in Virginia used a breeches buoy to remove thirteen crew members from a freighter (at right) driven aground during a hurricane in 1944.

Outside the 12-mile limit, the 293-foot former navy destroyer Terry *pickets the suspected rumrunner* Mistinguette. *Picketing duty wore out many Coast Guard vessels, including the* Terry, *retired in 1931.*

One thousand sacks of liquor, valued at more than $50,000, were confiscated from the notorious rumrunner Baboon *(part of deck shown here) after her capture by the Coast Guard in December 1931.*

Faced with capture by a Coast Guard vessel, the crew of the rumrunner Linwood *set her afire to destroy her cargo of liquor.*

The Loening OL-5 amphibian was the first aircraft purchased especially for Coast Guard use. It had a cruising speed of 75 mph and a range of 415 miles. No. 1, shown here, was delivered in October, 1926. Three OL-5's were in service at the year's end.

The First Coast Guard Aviation Group posed for this photograph at the Naval Air Station, Pensacola, Florida, where the men received their training.

*During World War II watchful coastguardsmen on antisub-
marine duty were responsible for the sinking of eleven submarines
and the rescue of four thousand survivors of torpedoings.*

Coast Guard landing barges delivered thousands of men to the invasion beaches. They were loaded from troop transports anchored offshore.

Loaded railroad cars moved across the English Channel in Coast Guard-manned LSTs. From the LST's deck, crewmen watch the cars roll away.

*A Coast Guard-manned transport is preparing to load German
prisoners for detention in the United States.*

Surrounded by congressmen and officials from the Treasury Department and the Coast Guard, President Harry S. Truman signs a bill defining the missions of the Coast Guard. The ceremony took place on August 4, 1949, the Coast Guard's 159th anniversary.

Long-range search and rescue missions are handled by the Coast Guard's 378-foot cutters, which also perform ocean station patrol, oceanographic research, and meteorology duties. The Sherman (below), named for John Sherman, secretary of the treasury from 1877 until 1881, was commissioned in 1968. She carries the latest rescue equipment, including a helicopter on her flight deck.

Making Money: The Bureau of Engraving and Printing

EACH YEAR THE UNITED STATES GOVERNMENT ISsues paper currency, bonds, notes and stamps worth many billions of dollars. These and other printed items of a financial character are produced by the Treasury's Bureau of Engraving and Printing. Although the bureau prints materials for seventy-five government departments and agencies, its principal product is paper currency—more than $2 billion worth annually at a rate of 12 million notes a day.

What was to become the Bureau of Engraving and Printing began operations in 1862 when two men and four women, working at presses installed in the basement of the Treasury building, overprinted the Treasury seal along with the signatures of the register of the Treasury and the treasurer of the United States on $1 and $2 notes. The notes had been plate-printed by private bank note companies after Congress, at the request of Secretary of the Treasury Salmon P. Chase, voted to issue paper money as a means of financing the Civil War.

Spencer Clark, the chief clerk of the Treasury's Bureau of Construction, made the suggestion that the notes be returned to the Treasury for overprinting, and he designed the seal that was added to the

A cartoon that appeared in the Brooklyn Eagle *in 1929 when the Bureau of Engraving and Printing began to turn out the new, small-sized currency.*

notes as evidence of lawful issue. A variation of the seal designed by Clark is still used on United States securities. In Clark's words the design had at its center a "facsimile of the seal adopted by the Treasury Department for its documents on a ground of geometriclathe work, the exterior being composed of thirty-four points, similarly executed. [A geometriclathe has a flexible cutting tool; it was used to engrave parts of the die for Clark's seal.] These points were designed to be typical of the thirty-four states, and to simulate the appearance of the seals ordinarily affixed to public documents." Loyal to the federal government, Clark ignored the Civil War and included a point in his design for each of the eleven states then in secession.

Secretary Chase placed Clark in charge of the Treasury's basement currency overprinting operation, directing Clark to "keep a daily record, in a book prepared for that purpose, of each day's work, and its cost, for which you will render a weekly statement, or if hereafter ordered, a daily statement." Chase continued: "You will, therefore, on and after Monday next, receive from the mail the one and two dollar notes, making the customary receipt thereof, and after sealing and trimming deliver them to the Treasurer, and take his receipt. You will keep a perfect record at every step, using all the checks and guards now used in the organization of the larger notes, with such additional checks as you may deem proper that do not involve additional cost, and may seem to you additional security. You will make a daily report of the amount of notes on hand, amount received from the engraver, the amount delivered to the Treasurer, and the amount in your hands at the close of work on each day, showing under each head the respective quantity of ones and twos, and also aggregating the total amounts of all bills received from the engravers up to the date of the report, with respective amounts of ones and twos."

Within a week Clark had obtained a steam engine and boiler and installed them, with other equipment, in the basement of the Treasury building. In one of his reports, Clark said of the beginning of his overprinting project: "On the 28th day of August, 1862, I commenced the work with one male assistant and four female operatives." Clark's success is attested by the assignment of the processing of all denominations of notes to the basement workroom in January 1863.

Meanwhile, Clark had been looking into the high prices charged the government by private bank note companies for printing currency notes. He informed Secretary Chase that notes could be produced in the Treasury Department "for a comparatively small out-

lay, at a great saving of cost in the issues." Acting on Clark's recommendation, the secretary asked Congress to authorize the engraving and printing of currency at the Treasury, and Congress gave its approval.

The data of the first plate printing of notes by the Treasury is in question. Charles Neale, a plate printer, had been brought into the department as a clerk in anticipation of authority to print currency. On October 11, 1862, he was appointed to superintend the plate-printing operation and was told to begin installing presses, obtaining ink and paper, and hiring workmen. Evidently, Neale had difficulty inducing printers to come to the Treasury. The printing of paper money by the government was something new. There were misgivings as to the success of the proposed printing venture, and even if it should be successful, many persons were doubtful of its permanency. Neale was instructed to have the men he hired report for duty any time after November 1, 1862, but on December 12, Clark wrote to Secretary Chase: "No printers are yet employed." According to one account, plate printing in the Treasury did not commence until the fall of 1863.

James Duthie, the bureau's first engraver, was a skilled craftsman. He served as superintendent of

This building, located at 14th and C streets S.W. in Washington, houses the headquarters of the Bureau of Engraving and Printing.

engraving until about 1865. Duthie's best known work was the dock scene used on all denominations of the first issue of fractional currency, the small denomination notes issued in place of coins during the Civil War and for some ten years afterward. The design depicted steamboats at the water's edge with gangplanks down, cargo piled high on the wharf, a horse-drawn dray awaiting unloading, and a smoking steam engine in the distance.

Hope for a quick end to the Civil War, expressed in President Lincoln's first call for volunteers to the number of only 75,000 for a ninety-day enlistment, had quickly faded with the initial defeats suffered by the Union forces, and worried citizens began to hoard coins. Thousands of dollars were removed from circulation each day. In one case, a house in New York City reportedly collapsed from the weight of the coins cached there.

In place of coins, privately issued tokens and scrip, the latter derisively termed "shinplaster" circulated, creating, in Secretary Chase's words, "a manifest necessity for a fractional currency authorized by the national government." In March 1863, Chase received permission to issue the small denomination notes, producing them in the Treasury Department as they were needed. The first notes, bearing Duthie's design, were issued in October 1863.

The face and back of the five-cent note of the first issue of fractional currency. It was printed in the Treasury building in 1863.

Secretary of the Treasury Salmon P. Chase. During his term in office (1861–1864) the Treasury began the currency overprinting that led to the establishment of the Bureau of Engraving and Printing.

In all, there were four issues of fractional currency. The first two were printed wholly in the Treasury building; private bank note companies did some of the work on the third and fourth issues. The second issue of fractional currency proved to be the most controversial. It introduced a new three-cent note, the lowest denomination of fractional currency, and doubt was expressed as to the actual need for it. There was another outcry because the portrait of Spencer Clark was used on the five-cent note, a selection that produced a running controversy in the columns of the *New York Times*. The dispute reached the floor of Congress and resulted in the passage of the law that remains in effect today, prohibiting the use of a portrait of any living person on a security of the United States. Although the use of Clark's portrait received much criticism, the fact that the likeness of Francis E. Spinner, the then very much alive treasurer of the United States, appeared on the fifty-cent note was ignored.

Fractional currency continued to be issued until 1876. The amount authorized was $50 million; however, the total quantity placed in circulation, including reissues, exceeded $368,720,000. Today, it is estimated that almost $2 million of these notes remain outstanding.

The controversial five-cent fractional currency note that carried the portrait of the director of the Treasury's printing operations, Spencer Clark, a selection that led to a congressional ban on the use of portraits of living persons on United States securities.

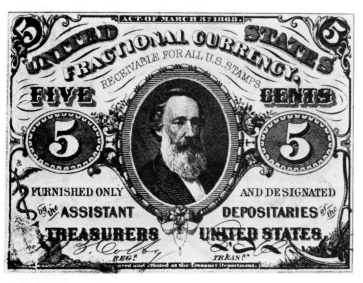

It was natural that there would be opposition to the printing of paper money by the United States Treasury. The system, as well as Spencer Clark, who was regarded as its progenitor, had detractors in Congress, in private business, especially among bank note companies, in the newspapers, and even among employees and officers of the department. Clark answered allegations in the *New York World* that an "extensive portion of the Treasury building" had been set apart as a printing establishment by citing the use of one room each in the attic, basement, and cellar for printing. He stated that the "costly purchases of machinery and materials" did not amount to $2,000, exclusive of a steam engine and boiler, and the hiring of a "small army of engravers and printers and other employees" involved only four engravers, no printers having been engaged up to that time.

But the demands placed on the Treasury by the war could only be met by hiring more workers. In 1861 the Treasury Department employed 380 clerks. By 1864 the number had increased to 2,000, the majority of them women, an unusual situation in the male-dominated government agencies of that day and the occasion for gossip when many of the new employees were assigned to the night shift. However, in 1864, after a two-month investigation, a committee of the House of Representatives found charges of immoralities to be baseless. Furthermore, the committee approved in principle of the Treasury's printing paper money and commended the way in which the department was doing the work.

When currency printing began in the Treasury building, Secretary Chase was well aware that distinctively marked paper, limited by law to use in printing currency, was a prime deterrent to counterfeiting. At his direction the department issued an advertisement inviting proposals from manufacturers to furnish paper to the Treasury. One of the responses was from Stuart Gwynn of Boston, Massachusetts, who submitted samples of a vegetable membrane paper described as being of "most extraordinary character and excellence." In Spencer Clark's opinion, Gwynn's distinctive mark was "ingenious and might be serviceable to the department in detecting counterfeits." Accordingly, in 1862, Gwynn received a contract to produce the unique paper in the Treasury Department. The paper could not be dissolved in hot or cold water; it could not be split; its fiber had an irremovable nonphotographic tint; and it took ink more readily, retained it longer, and was reported to be better than any paper manufactured for currency in any country.

Under the terms of the contract, the department had the exclusive right to produce Gwynn's paper, and the secret manufacturing process was not to be divulged to anyone except those immediately engaged in producing the paper in the Treasury building. Gwynn was also required to superintend the construction of the necessary machinery for the manufacture of the paper.

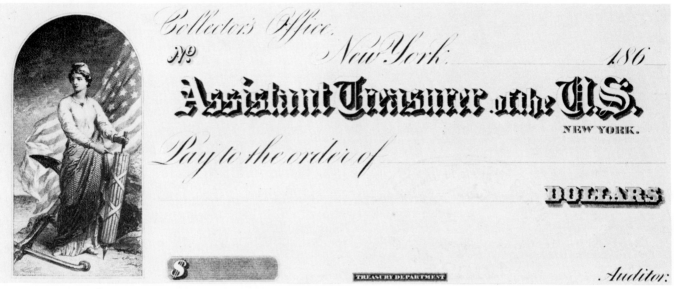

Government checks similar to this one were an important product of the Treasury Department's first presses. The check was printed in a green color from a die prepared by the American Bank Note Company.

This engraving carried the title "Making Money. The Room in the Treasury Building Where the Greenbacks Are Printed."

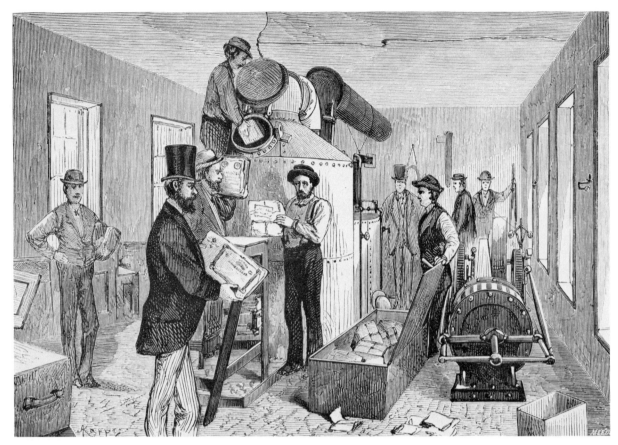

Treasury employees are destroying worn and defaced currency. The engraving, captioned "Burnt to Ashes. The End of Uncle Sam's Greenbacks," was accompanied by the information that burning took place every day at twelve o'clock.

A contemporary artist produced this engraving of Treasury clerks at work during the Civil War years.

A hand printing press. In 1864 the Treasury reported ninety-six hand presses in use.

An artist's rendering of the Treasury's hydrostatic pressroom. The Treasury began to use presses operated by hydraulic pressure during the Civil War years.

The famous Civil War photographer Mathew Brady took this picture of the currency pressroom located in the attic of the Treasury building.

In 1878 the Bureau of Engraving and Printing received its first steam-powered printing press. Early models, similar to this one, were used to print tobacco stamps and the green-colored backs of some United States notes.

Another artist's rendering of the Treasury's Civil War–era currency operations depicts the room where a force of women applied the finishing touches to paper money. The ladies seated in the gallery on the right were examiners.

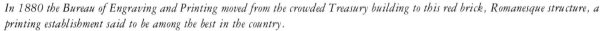

In 1880 the Bureau of Engraving and Printing moved from the crowded Treasury building to this red brick, Romanesque structure, a printing establishment said to be among the best in the country.

The Bureau of Engraving and Printing appears in the background of this 1890 photo showing a bureau wagon taking finished bills to the Treasury building.

The bureau's main plate-printing pressroom at the time of the Spanish-American War. The paddles near the ceiling circulated the air in the room.

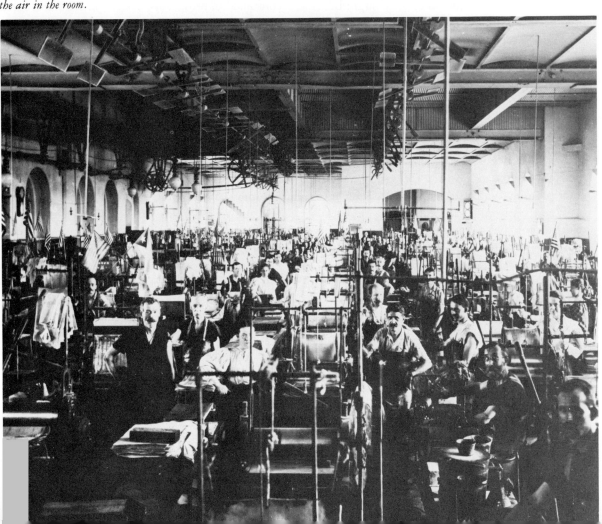

Thus, the United States Treasury acquired its first distinctive paper for currency. Originally intended for all note issues, the paper had been used only in the production of fractional currency when a disagreement between the Treasury and the supplier of the basic paper stock brought the manufacture of the special paper to a temporary halt. Meanwhile, Gwynn was imprisoned on charges of defrauding the government, charges which later were proven unfounded. Gwynn then disassociated himself from the Treasury project, leaving the execution of his contract to a subordinate and an attorney. Without Gwynn's personal direction, however, the manufacture of the paper lagged and was soon discontinued.

Distinctive paper for currency was not used again until 1869 when Secretary George S. Boutwell entered into a contract with a Philadelphia company. In 1879 the Treasury awarded a contract to Crane & Co. of Dalton, Massachusetts, a firm that supplied a paper "of pure linen stock, with continuous colored (red and blue) silk lines or threads running parallel to each other from the top to the bottom of each sheet, or from side to side, as the case might be; and in addition, thereto, colored (red and blue) silk fibres were introduced into the pulp from which the paper was made."

Although the distinctive features and basic rag content of the paper it uses have changed over the years, usually as a result of wartime shortages or technological advances, the Treasury has continued to purchase special paper from private contractors.

The Treasury's use of green ink, rather than black, or another color, for printing the backs of currency notes probably can be traced to the fact that private bank note companies had developed a special green ink that could be used when the front of the note was printed with a black ink. The use of two colors made bills harder to counterfeit, but ordinary ink on the back had a tendency to strike through to the opposite side of the bill. By printing the back of the bill in the specially developed shade of green the strike-through was made less noticeable. When it took over currency production, the Treasury used green for the backs of its notes for the sake of uniformity. Later, in the absence of a good reason for changing colors, the production of "greenbacks" continued.

The same desperate need for Civil War financing that led to the printing of paper money by the Treasury Department also led to the production of revenue stamps "for expressing and denoting the several stamp duties" levied by a newly appointed commissioner of internal revenue. Medicines, perfumes, cosmetics, playing cards, tobacco, liquors, beer and other products, and certain commercial papers were subject to stamp taxes.

Although the bulk of the printing of the first revenue stamps was contracted to private firms, the Treasury printed beer and cigar stamps as early as 1867. The next few years saw an increase in the number of revenue stamps printed and processed by the Treasury. An annual report for fiscal year 1870 indicates deliveries of 31 million stamps for distilled spirits, beer, tobacco, custom cigars, and certain other taxed products. By 1873 deliveries had risen to over 224 million stamps and the categories had expanded to include distilled spirits for export, compound liquor, cigars, cigarettes, and snuff. Much of the printing had reverted to private bank note companies by 1875 since their bids for producing stamps were usually less than those of the bureau, which continued to print only the custom cigar and special tax stamps. An act appropriating funds for government expenses for fiscal year 1877 required that internal revenue stamps be printed in the bureau, provided that the cost did not exceed what was being paid under existing contracts to private companies. However, the secretary of the treasury felt that the bureau would be unable to compete with the private firms and it was not until the following year, under a new secretary, that the bureau resumed manufacture of almost all internal revenue stamps.

From the beginning currency and revenue-stamp printing operations had been carried out in whatever space could be found in the Treasury building. Spencer Clark had complained that 237 male and 288 female employees and a "total of 324 engines, machines, etc." were crowded into inadequte work space in the basement and the attic of the building, an arrangement that required the use of a dumbwaiter to transport paper and printed securities between the two locations.

However, it was 1878 before a site was finally purchased for a new Bureau of Engraving and Printing building, but once that step had been taken construction quickly got under way. The new building, Romanesque in style and located near the

Washington Monument, opened its doors on July 1, 1880. Its presence brought changes to the semirural area that surrounded it. Dirt roads became cobblestone streets on which dray teams replaced farm horses. Pasture land developed into city blocks with row houses. Along with these changes, surrounding land values soared.

During the 1880s and 1890s the economic growth of the nation created an ever-increasing demand for the products of the Bureau of Engraving and Printing. In 1891, 21 percent more notes and stamps were printed than in the previous year and production continued to increase. Within a decade the workload of the bureau outgrew the capacity of its new building. Contributing to this predicament were the restrictions imposed by Congress on the use of steam-powered presses, which resulted in the replacement of nineteen steam presses with some sixty-odd hand presses. Already inadequate bureau facilities became exceedingly overcrowded with the installation of hand presses and the additional workers needed to operate them.

Congress voted funds for a new wing for the Bureau of Engraving and Printing in 1890; an extension to house a boiler plant was added in 1894; and in 1900 Congress authorized the construction of a second wing and an outbuilding to house an ink mill, carpenter shop, harness room, stable, and coal storage facilities. The bureau acquired a new laundry and stable in 1904 and still another addition the next year.

The constant need for expansion was only one of the problems facing the bureau. Its red brick building had been hailed as one of the country's most modern printing facilities when it opened in 1880. By the turn of the century, however, technological changes had made it obsolete and bureau officials began to think in terms of a new building.

Meanwhile, in 1894, the bureau had expanded its activities to include the printing of postage stamps previously produced for the Post Office Department by private bank note companies. The first stamp printed by the bureau, a reddish brown, six-cent stamp, reached the nation's post offices in July 1894. A four-cent stamp followed, and by the end of its first year of stamp operations, the bureau had printed more than 21 million sheets of stamps, including thirteen denominations of ordinary postage stamps and special delivery, postage due, and newspaper and periodical stamps.

Bureau of Engraving and Printing officials who had complained of overcrowding before they began to print stamps now urgently requested "an entirely new building for the Bureau, to be designed and constructed for its special needs." In 1914 they moved into a modern plant with ten acres of floor space. The structure, fronting on Washington's Fifteenth Street with four 296-foot factory wings extending toward Fourteenth Street, continues to house bureau activities.

For the World's Columbian Exposition held in Chicago in 1895 the Bureau of Engraving and Printing turned out 25,000 copies of this diploma. The bureau proudly reported that the diploma, which was presented to exhibitors, had been praised as "one of the most beautiful and skillfully executed works of its kind ever issued."

Wetting paper prior to printing.

Trimming currency.

Examining completed stamps.

Separating, counting, and packaging currency.

Laundering soiled currency.

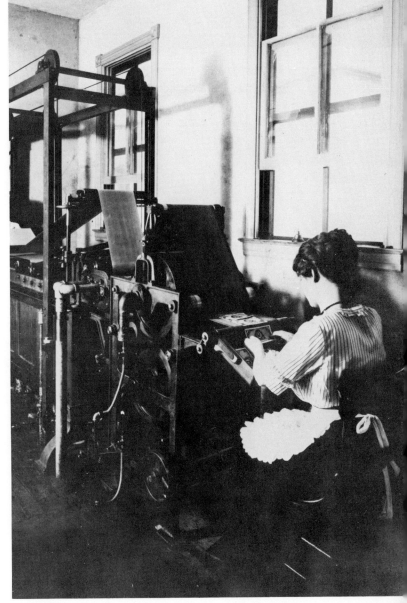

Currency is being transferred under heavy guard from a vault in the Bureau of Engraving and Printing to the Treasury building.

A group of Bureau of Engraving and Printing employees departing for the opening game of the 1905 baseball season.

The four factory wings of the Bureau of Engraving and Printing building as they appeared in 1914 when the facility opened.

"Protection of American Womanhood" was the theme of this Bureau of Engraving and Printing float that won a prize in Washington's 1916 Preparedness Parade.

These bureau employees marched in the parade.

World War I further expanded the Bureau of Engraving and Printing's workload. In November 1918, the month the war ended, there were 8,432 persons on the payroll, the largest number ever employed by the bureau.

Probably the bureau's most noteworthy achievement during the war years was the printing and processing of five issues of Liberty Loan bonds. Issued to finance the war effort, more than 100 million bonds were printed from April 1917 through the spring of 1919. The demand for bonds and other materials for war-financing programs forced the bureau to hire 1,200 additional people and adopt a twenty-four-hour daily work schedule. The unprecedented workload also opened the way to the full use of power plate-printing presses, formerly restricted by law to the printing of postage and internal revenue stamps and to a few steps in the printing of currency and bonds. In 1923, the theory that the products of power presses were inferior to those of hand-roller presses having been disproved, Congress lifted all restrictions on the use of power presses.

Smaller-sized currency notes, under consideration by Treasury officials for many years, made their appearance in 1929. In spite of arguments that printing notes of a smaller size would save the government over $600,000 annually, proposals to reduce the size of paper money made little headway at first. The idea was not completely forgotten, however. In 1925 Secretary of the Treasury Andrew Mellon appointed a committee to restudy the whole question of currency design, printing operations, and other matters related to the replacing of large-sized currency with smaller notes. The committee recommended Washington's portrait for the new, smaller $1 note because the first president was familiar to everyone and bills of this denomination had the greatest circulation. Garfield's likeness was suggested for the $2 bill because of the sentiment attached to martyred presidents and because his flowing beard, in marked contrast to the clean-shaven features of Washington, would allow a ready distinction between the $1 and $2 bills. Lincoln's portrait was suggested for the $5 bill because he followed

In 1918 Bureau of Engraving and Printing employees organized a brass band.

Washington in the rank of American heroes and it seemed logical that his likeness should appear on the denomination having the second largest circulation. The committee's recommendations were approved by Secretary Mellon in 1927.

At the Bureau of Engraving and Printing the change to smaller-sized notes meant that new dies, rolls, and plates had to be made. The reduced size permitted the printing of twelve notes with each plate instead of eight as was the case with most of the large notes. The bureau had no difficulty in converting its plate-printing equipment, but trimming machines used to remove excess margins from the printed sheets had to be rebuilt and machines utilizing a new method of numbering notes had to be designed and installed.

A workable system for numbering paper money requires that there be no two notes of any one class, denomination, and series with the same identification number in order that the record of a note's production may be traced at any time. The system must be able to accommodate a large volume of notes, and

the size of the type used for the numbers must be sufficiently large to facilitate immediate identification. The ingenious machines developed at the Bureau of Engraving and Printing were able to cut twelve-note sheets in half lengthwise, overprint each note with its number and the Treasury seal, cut the half sheets into individual notes, and dispense the notes in reverse numerical order.

Prior to the introduction of the new currency, the Treasury had to accumulate sufficient quantities of notes to provide for the simultaneous issue of the various classes and denominations. Notes in denominations from $1 to $20 were printed first; the higher denominations of gold certificates and Federal Reserve currency followed along with the established denominations of national bank notes. Also before introducing the new currency, the Treasury launched a vigorous campaign to familiarize the public with the notes to be issued. Banks across the nation displayed the new bills, and speakers were sent out to explain how the change in currency was to be accomplished.

Below this model of a proposed design for the back of the series 1935 $1 note are President Franklin D. Roosevelt's scratched-through signature and his suggestions for changes.

For the Bureau of Engraving and Printing the introduction of the new small-sized currency was the most radical production change in its history. However, the bureau successfully handled the conversion to the new notes, which began to circulate in July 1929.

Although the events were unrelated, the appearance of the first small-sized notes was closely followed by the collapse of the New York stock market and the great depression of the 1930s. During the depression years the Bureau of Engraving and Printing, operating with a reduced work force, printed special currency, checks, and bonds for use in connection with recovery projects. In 1935 the bureau began to print United States savings bonds, introduced that year to attract the small investor and still produced today.

At the suggestion of President Franklin D. Roosevelt, the Post Office Department, in 1938, issued the first of the postage stamps that came to be known as the presidential series. The basic design for the series was selected after a national competition, the first such competition ever held for a postage stamp design. Because the winning entry, out of 1,027 designs submitted, depicted a bust of George Washington in profile position, the Bureau of Engraving and Printing had to locate sculptures that would be suitable for copying in preparing the designs for the stamps honoring the other presidents. Sculptured likenesses were located for all the presidents with the exception of President Taft; the design of his stamp was based on a profile photograph. Eleven of the presidential likenesses were copied from medals struck by the Treasury's Bureau of the Mint. The only ex-president not included in the series was Herbert Hoover, an omission made necessary by the federal statute prohibiting the likeness of a living person from appearing on a United States security.

The Post Office Department's Famous Americans series of postage stamps, inaugurated in 1940, provided the Bureau of Engraving and Printing's research staff with another important project. The series honored thirty-five illustrious Americans in the arts and sciences. Stamp designs were based on portraits of the honorees, preferably depicting them in their most productive years.

During World War II the Bureau of Engraving and Printing, by then operating in an annex building as well as in its main building, printed, first, de-

A model of the revised design incorporating the president's recommendation carries his signature of approval along with that of Secretary of the Treasury Henry Morgenthau, Jr.

fense savings bonds and, after the United States entered the conflict, war savings bonds. The bureau also printed ten-cent savings stamps carrying a reproduction of Daniel Chester French's statue *The Minute Man*. The stamps could be used to purchase bonds.

Special wartime currencies produced by the Bureau of Engraving and Printing included United States money for circulation in Hawaii and military and occupational currency for use in Italy, France, Austria, Germany, and Japan. The bureau also produced Philippine currency for military operations in the Philippine Islands.

During the war years the Bureau of Engraving and Printing was closed to visitors. A ban on sightseers had also been in effect during World War I. At other times, however, the bureau was, and continues to be, one of Washington's most popular tourist attractions. Spencer Clark, the bureau's first chief, had complained about the disruptions caused by visitors. "I see nothing to commend the practice," he wrote to the secretary of the treasury. "It would not be permitted in any other branch of the public service where valuables were handled." Clark recommended that sightseers be prohibited as a "serious hindrance to the public business." Nevertheless, the public, fascinated with the bureau's moneymaking activities, continued to visit, although a Washington guidebook published in 1874 indicates that admission was by a pass obtained from the secretary of the treasury.

Clark's successors also had trouble with visitors. In 1875 George B. McCartee complained of the loss of two sheets of $10 notes worth $80 "from theft perpetrated by visitors to the Bureau." In 1880 rules issued for bureau guides and visitors limited visitors to thirty at a time and prohibited conversation with employees and the handling of "impressions, plates, or representations of value." By 1900 restrictions had been relaxed somewhat, and when the bureau's new building opened in 1914, it provided mezzanines in the various workrooms from which visitors could view moneymaking operations.

Although the bureau's strict accounting procedures during the manufacture of securities keep losses at a minimum, shortages have occurred from time to time. From the earliest days of the bureau, if a shortage could be traced to a particular employee,

that person had to make good the loss. If the shortage could not be traced to one employee or to a group of employees, all the workers in the section or division where the shortage occured were assessed for the amount of the loss. Over the years a system developed whereby bureau employees made contributions to a special fund that was used to make up any shortages. The special fund was discontinued in 1951, but in cases where responsibility can be fixed, bureau employees are still held liable for losses if the government is called upon to redeem the securities in question.

The Bureau of Engraving and Printing's biggest shortage occurred in 1954 when, on the first workday of the year, two packages containing a total of $160,000 in $20 Federal Reserve notes were discovered to be missing from the vault in which they had been stored after being wrapped in heavy paper and labeled. They had been replaced by two dummy packages wrapped to resemble the genuine packages of notes, which the bureau calls "bricks." The substitution was discovered when bureau employees, working in the vault, noticed that two bricks were suspiciously light in weight. Upon being opened, the packages were found to contain ordinary paper cut into the size of currency notes.

Secret Service agents, charged with protecting the nation's currency, began an immediate investigation. Their efforts and a report from the Virginia State Police that many of the missing notes had been

The prizewinning design for the 1938 presidential series of postage stamps.

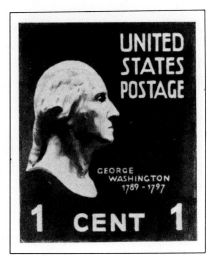

found on a farm in that state led to a speedy solution of the case and to the arrest of a currency wrapper named James Landis who was convicted of the theft of the two bundles of $20 bills.

At home, Landis had cut up paper into pieces the size of currency notes and packaged them to resemble regular bureau work. He placed the bundles in a bag and brought them to the bureau on the morning of December 30. Upon entering the building, he approached the parcel booth, ostensibly to check his bag in accordance with regulations that prohibit the taking of unexamined items into workrooms. Waiting until the guard at the door turned his attention to other employees, Landis slipped by the parcel booth and carried his bag to a locker room on the third floor where, unnoticed, he concealed it under a burlap bag suspended in a large trash can. He then went to his own locker room, changed into his work clothes, and reported for work at the usual time.

Landis's first assignment that morning was to assemble banded currency notes on a skid and deliver them to the wrapping machine. From previous experience he knew that it would take about twenty minutes to wrap the quantity of notes he had delivered. During that twenty minutes he walked over to a skid that held already wrapped currency, picked up two packages, covered them with paper, and carried them out of the room to a storage area in the attic. There he tore off the wrappers and steel bands and placed the money in two paper bags he had brought along for that purpose. He concealed the bags under some rubbish but retained the labels that bore package and serial numbers. Because Landis was back on the first floor before it was time to bring more work to the wrapping machine, his absence went unnoticed. Later that morning, during his regular rest period, he returned to the third-floor locker room, placed the labels under hot water to separate them from the paper to which they were glued, and pasted them onto his false packages that he had retrieved from the trash can. He then covered the packages with a piece of paper, took them to the packaging room, and placed them on the skid of finished work. The loaded skid was later removed to the vault.

That afternoon, his tour of duty completed, Landis changed into street clothes, went up to the attic, and picked up one of the paper bags that he had hidden there; it contained $128,000, as much as he thought he could carry out of the building at one time. Placing his soiled work clothes on top of the stolen bills, Landis made his way to the employee's exit. On the way out he pulled a trouser leg from the bag to indicate to the guard that it contained soiled clothing. The usual security check was made in the operating section at the end of the day, but all labeled packages were accounted for and there was no cause for suspicion.

Things were different, however, after the dummy packages were discovered in the vault. Secret Service agents interviewed all employees who had access to the processing section where the missing notes had been handled. The investigators were able to link Landis to the notes found in Virginia and his arrest followed. The government recovered approximately $132,840 of the stolen money and collected an additional $2,000 from retirement funds and salary payments due Landis.

Like any successful manufacturing establishment, the Bureau of Engraving and Printing continually improves the materials and processes used by its highly skilled artists, engravers, and plate printers to produce paper currency and other items that meet the highest standards. Ninety-nine percent of the currency produced by the bureau consists of Federal Reserve notes, issued in denominations of $1, $2, $5, $20, $50, and $100 by Federal Reserve banks. The bureau also turns out $100 United States notes, which are issued by the Treasury. Prior to 1969 the bureau printed $500, $1,000, $5,000, and $10,000 notes. The largest denomination ever to come off the presses was the $100,000 gold certificate of 1934, but it was designed for official transactions and never circulated outside of Federal Reserve banks. Production of $2 United States notes was discontinued in 1966. The $2 bill now in circulation is a Federal Reserve note introduced in 1976.

When a new currency note is under consideration, the secretary of the treasury selects its design after conferring with the director of the Bureau of Engraving and Printing, the treasurer of the United States, the board of governors of the Federal Reserve System, and other interested officials. Then, using delicate cutting instruments, called gravers, and powerful magnifying glasses, the bureau's expert engravers cut features of the chosen design in varying depths into soft steel dies. Each element, such as the por-

Artists.

Authors.

Composers.

Educators.

Stamps in the Famous Americans series.

trait, the vignette, the numerals, the lettering, the script, and the scrollwork, is engraved by a different craftsman who has spent years learning his trade. The several dies that make up a design are united in their proper positions in the process of preparing plates for printing.

To ensure the best protection against counterfeiting, paper currency and most postage stamps are printed by the intaglio process. Especially in the case of the portrait, the slightest variation in the breadth, spacing, or depth of line of a counterfeit bill can be detected when compared with a genuine intaglio-printed note. The bureau's high-speed, sheet-fed rotary presses accommodate either two or four plates of thirty-two notes, called subjects, each. They print eight thousand sheets per hour. In the intaglio printing process each sheet is forced, under very heavy pressure, into the fine lines of an engraved plate to pick up a special ink developed in the bureau's laboratories. The backs of the notes are

Inventors.

Poets.

Scientists.

Workers in the Bureau of Engraving and Printing's War Bond section during World War II.

Enlarged one and one-half times, this ten-lire note is an example of the Allied military currency produced by the Bureau of Engraving and Printing during World War II.

printed with green ink one day and the faces with black ink the following day.

After the printing operation, the thirty-two-subject sheets are examined for defects before being cut into sixteen-subject size and overprinted with the Treasury seal, serial numbers, and a Federal Reserve district seal and number. At this point examiners check the notes again. If a note is found to be imperfect, it is replaced with a "star" note. Star notes are exactly like the notes they replace except that they carry an independent series of serial numbers. On Federal Reserve notes a star appears instead of the usual suffix letter; on United States notes a star replaces the prefix letter. The serial number of an imperfect note is not used again in the same numbering sequence.

The automated equipment that performs the overprinting also gathers sixteen-subject sheets into stacks of a hundred sheets and conveys them to cutting knives that divide the sheets into pairs of notes and then into individual notes. Units of a hundred notes are banded and packaged into bricks weighing about eight and one half pounds. After a final inspection, the bricks are compressed, banded, plastic shrink-wrapped, and placed in pouches for shipment to one of the twelve Federal Reserve districts where they are used primarily to replace worn or mutilated currency taken out of circulation.

Each year the presses of the Bureau of Engraving and Printing turn out approximately 27 billion United States postage stamps including the regular series of stamps that are kept in constant supply at post offices, stamps for extra services, such as special delivery, stamps for special occasions, such as Christmas, memorial stamps honoring American statesmen (usually presidents) who die in office, and commemorative stamps honoring important people and events.

Developing a new stamp design is the responsibility of the United States Postal Service. The Bureau of Engraving and Printing enters the picture when its artists prepare the models from which the final design selection is made. The bureau then makes plates from the approved model and prints the stamps on its presses using the intaglio process for single color stamps. Multicolor stamps are produced on intaglio presses and by other methods depending on the number of colors, the size of the stamp and its design, and the type of issue. Some of the bureau's presses print stamps on pre-gummed paper; others apply the adhesive to the back of the stamps at the conclusion of the printing process. Most stamps also receive an invisible coating of phosphor which, when exposed to ultraviolet light, enables high-speed mail processing machines to cancel stamps automatically.

Postage stamps undergo a careful inspection for color, printing, gumming, and perforating defects before they leave the Bureau of Engraving and Printing. They are delivered to the Postal Service in sheet, book, and coil forms.

In all, the Bureau of Engraving and Printing turns out some eight hundred different products. In addition to the large-scale operations involved in currency and postage stamp production, the list includes United States bonds, revenue stamps, food coupons, and such diverse items as White House invitations, identification cards, commissions, diplomas, and certificates.

While the bureau was printing military currency for use in Italy, Italian counterfeiters were turning out bogus United States notes. This illicit press was discovered in Milan.

From one of the Bureau of Engraving and Printing's mezzanine galleries, visitors watch currency examiners at work.

This is how wrapped and labeled packages of currency were delivered to Bureau of Engraving and Printing vaults at the time of the big robbery on December 30, 1953.

Plate hardening—a step in the currency-making process.

Left: *A Bureau of Engraving and Printing craftsman transfers a steel die to a steel roll.* Right: *Transferring a steel roll to a steel plate.*

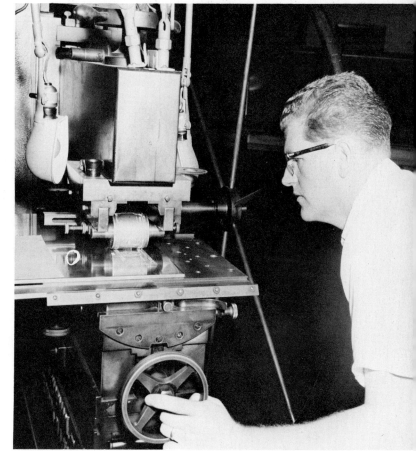

A bureau engraver at work on a plate from which currency will be printed.

One of the Bureau of Engraving and Printing's intaglio presses.

The final printing operation for paper currency, the overprinting of the Treasury seal, serial numbers, Federal Reserve district seal, and Federal Reserve district number, is accomplished by this machine. Called COPE (for Currency Overprinting and Processing Equipment), it performs the overprinting and then cuts, counts, bands, and packages the finished notes.

This bale of special currency paper is bound for the bureau's printing section.

Before the process was automated, sheets of currency were trimmed by hand.

Examiners play an important role in currency production; they are checking half sheets of $1 bills.

Reproduced here, the obverse with the likeness of Woodrow Wilson and the reverse of the $100,000 gold certificate of 1934, the largest denomination to come off the Bureau of Engraving and Printing's presses.

By June 1976 the Bureau of Engraving and Printing had produced 400 million of the $2 bills introduced in April of that year. The face of the note carries a likeness of Thomas Jefferson based on a portrait by Gilbert Stuart. The reverse shows the signing of the Declaration of Independence.

This product of the Bureau of Engraving and Printing is considered by many philatelists to be the most beautiful United States postage stamp of the nineteenth century. It bears the legend "Western Cattle in Storm."

These bureau employees are stacking sheets of newly gummed postage stamps. This photo was taken in 1903.

A Bureau of Engraving and Printing designer works on what will become a model for a postage stamp.

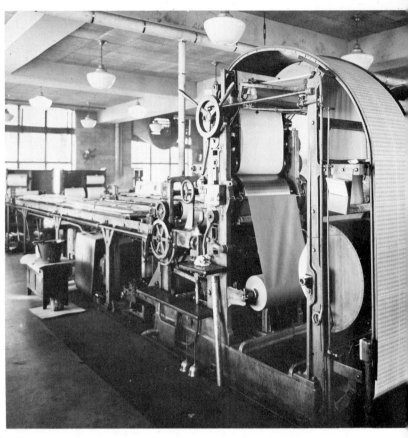

To meet an ever-increasing demand for stamps, the Bureau of Engraving and Printing has made many improvements in its printing presses. Left: What was then an innovative rotary web-fed intaglio press developed by Benjamin A. Stickney, a bureau employee, and introduced in 1914. Right: The Stickney press as it appeared when it was phased out in the early 1950s.

This engraver was photographed as he prepared the die for the three-cent International Red Cross commemorative stamp issued in 1952.

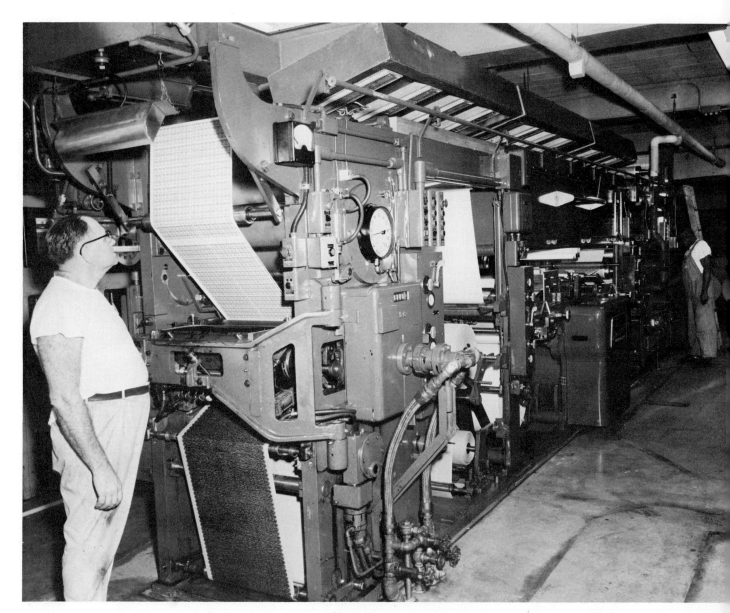

One of the stamp presses that replaced the bureau's old Stickney presses. Its speed and production were three times greater than that of a Stickney press.

UNITED STATES TREASURY DEPARTMENT
BUREAU OF ENGRAVING AND PRINTING

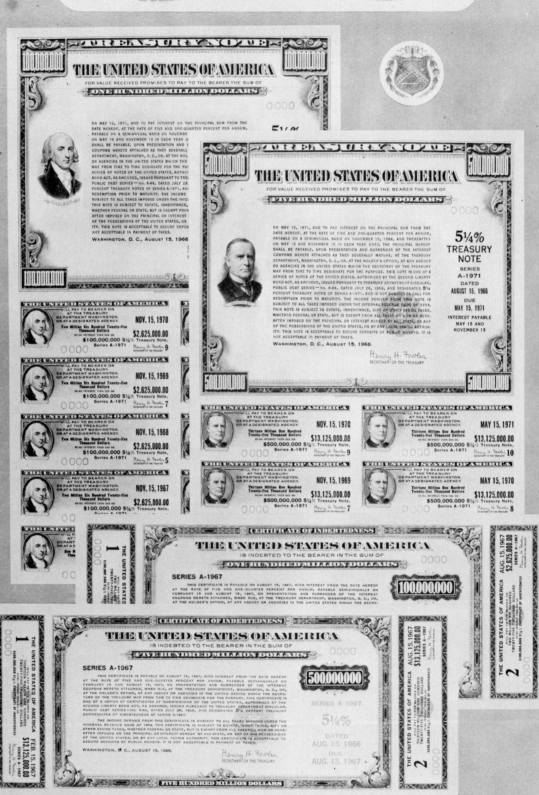

Managing the Nation's Finances:
The Fiscal Service

Two of the Treasury's bureaus act as its financial agents. They are the Bureau of Government Financial Operations and the Bureau of Public Debt; together they comprise the Fiscal Service of the Treasury Department.

The functions performed by the Bureau of Government Financial Operations are as old as the Treasury itself. The Act of Congress that created the Treasury Department also provided for a system of receiving, safeguarding, and paying out public money. In addition, Congress directed the secretary of the treasury to maintain an accounting system that would keep track of the federal government's receipts and expenditures. Because the legislators stipulated that a treasurer was to "receive and keep all moneys of the United States," in the beginning the treasurer of the United States had custody of whatever funds were in the national coffers. As a safeguard, however, the accounts were kept by an official known as the register of the treasury.

Over the years the steady expansion of the government's financial activities was reflected by changes in the Treasury Department. In 1894 the department established a separate division to handle

The $500-million and $100-million bonds pictured here were printed by the Bureau of Engraving and Printing.

the accounts formerly kept by the register. The new division also prepared an annual report for Congress showing the receipts and expenditures of the federal government. In 1920 these activities, along with the supervision of the deposit of public funds, were assigned to the newly created Office of the Commissioner of Accounts. It, in turn, was replaced by the Bureau of Accounts, a component of the Fiscal Service of the Treasury, established in 1940 by the president's Reorganization Plan. The Office of the Treasurer of the United States also became part of the Fiscal Service as did the Treasury's Division of Disbursement.

In its present form, the Bureau of Government Financial Operations dates from 1974 when the Treasury Department underwent still another reorganization. It involved the transfer of the position of treasurer of the United States to the Office of the Secretary and the assignment of the treasurer's operating functions and those of the Bureau of Accounts to the new Bureau of Government Financial Operations.

Almost every American, at one time or another, comes into contact with the Treasury's Bureau of Government Financial Operations. It is the agency that issues Treasury checks, more than 600 million of them annually, for federal salaries and wages, for goods and services purchased by the federal government, and for Social Security and veterans' benefits.

The bureau also reconciles all the checks that it issues against the accounts of government disbursing officers and investigates claims for checks that are cashed with forged endorsements, or are lost, stolen, or destroyed.

As the custodian of federal accounting records, the bureau issues regular reports on the government's cash assets and liabilities. It also reports on the status of appropriations approved by Congress and issues a daily report on deposits and withdrawals in the government's bank accounts, a monthly report on the amount of United States currency and coin in circulation, and a monthly report that shows the surplus or deficit in the president's budget. In addition, the Bureau of Government Financial Operations administers the deposit of withheld federal income taxes. It handles the government's investment accounts, pays claims against the government, and performs a variety of other services including the examination of partially destroyed United States currency to determine its value.

The other component of the Treasury's Fiscal Service, the Bureau of Public Debt, administers the federal government's debt, which on April 1, 1977, totaled $661 billion. An annual average interest rate of 6.449 percent is paid on that sum.

Although its public debt did not exceed $50 billion until World War II, the United States has always had a debt. In fact, having assumed the war debts of the former colonies, the nation began its existence owing money. The first attempt by Congress to manage the national debt came in the Funding Act of 1790, which provided for a loan commissioner in each of the states. In 1817 the duties of loan commissioners were transferred to the second Bank of the United States and in 1836 they were assumed by the secretary of the treasury. By 1836, however, the nation's interest-bearing debt had been discharged.

When the Civil War began in 1861, the federal government once again became a borrower and, for the first time, Congress authorized the secretary of

Left: The document setting up a $150,000 bond for Samuel Meredith when he assumed custody of United States funds in 1789. Right: A report in which the register of the Treasury, in charge of keeping the Treasury's account books, certifies that United States Treasurer Meredith had a balance of $562,731.18 in his account on October 1, 1791, and that the balance remained unchanged on December 31, 1791.

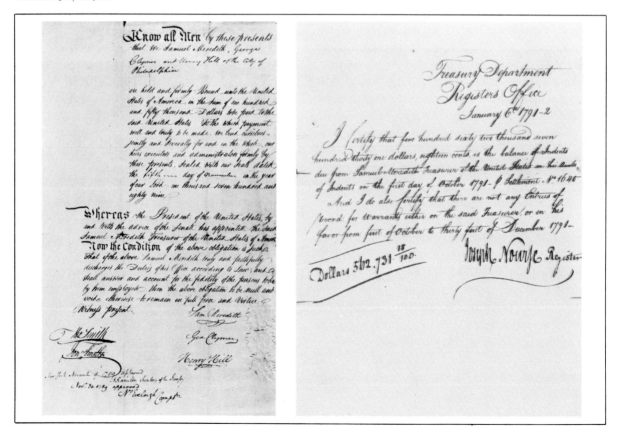

the treasury to issue securities to raise money. The secretary, Salmon P. Chase, established a Division of Loans for this purpose. That division was later combined with the Division of Currency to form the Division of Loans and Currency, which, with the Office of the Register of the Treasury, carried out the Treasury's public debt functions.

Expanded government borrowing to finance World War I led to the consolidation of the several agencies concerned with the national debt into the Public Debt Service under the direction of a Commissioner of the Public Debt. The service became the Bureau of Public Debt and a part of the Treasury's Fiscal Service in 1940.

When the government borrows money by issuing bonds and other public debt securities, the offering circulars are prepared by the Bureau of Public Debt; the bureau also directs the handling of security sales and it is responsible for the regulations governing United States security transactions. It also keeps records showing the owners of registered United States securities and authorizes interest payments when they are due. And when United States securities are lost, stolen, destroyed, or mutilated, claims are examined by bureau experts to determine if the securities should be replaced.

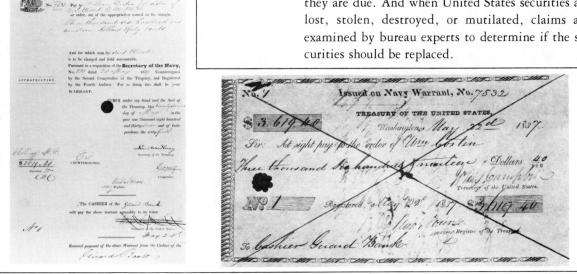

Left: *A Treasury Department warrant issued in 1837 authorizing the treasurer of the United States to pay $3619.40 to William Costin for uniforms supplied to the navy.* Right: *A photo of the Treasury check given to Mr. Costin.*

An example of a Treasury check used in the 1870s. It carries the portrait of Treasurer of the United States Francis E. Spinner.

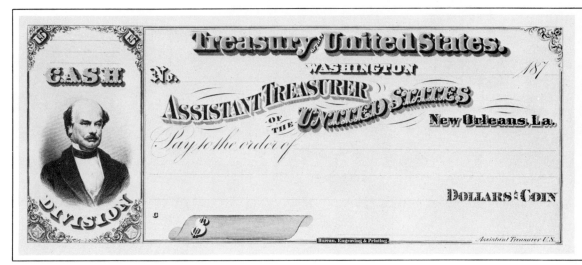

The room in the United States treasurer's Currency Redemption Division where worn-out bills were sorted and counted, seen here in a 1910 photograph.

The worker seated at the table is canceling worn-out bills by punching four holes into them.

A close-up of Redemption Division employees at work.

For a brief period the overprinting of serial numbers and the Treasury seal on United States currency was the responsibility of the United States treasurer. This is the room where the work was done.

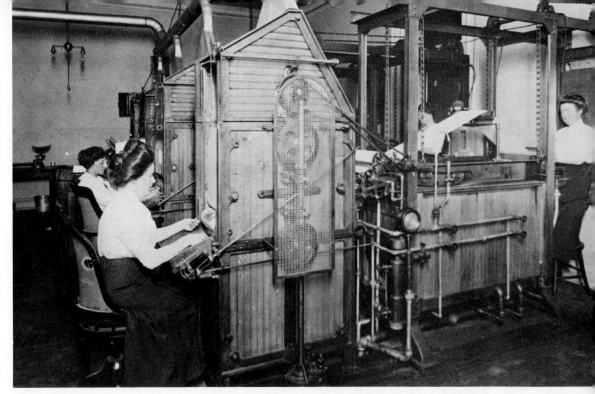

Currency that was soiled, but not damaged, was washed in these Redemption Division machines and put back into circulation.

Employees of the Bureau of Public Debt's Loans and Currency Division are counting unfit bills sent to them by the Redemption Division of the United States Treasurer's Office.

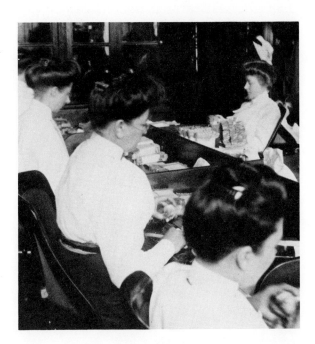

The Bureau of Public Debt's canceling room as it appeared in 1907. A hand-lettered sign on the wall says: "No smoking in this room or spitting on the floor."

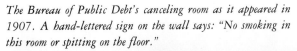

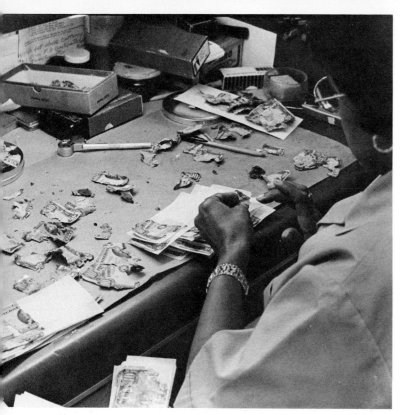

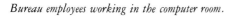

The Bureau of Government Financial Operations uses computers to carry out its numerous accounting and reporting activities. This photo was taken in the computer room.

In this contemporary photo a Bureau of Government Financial Operations expert is examining fragments of damaged money sent in for redemption. If more than one-half of the original note remains, it can be redeemed.

Charred bonds undergo examination by Bureau of Public Debt experts.

Bureau employees working in the computer room.

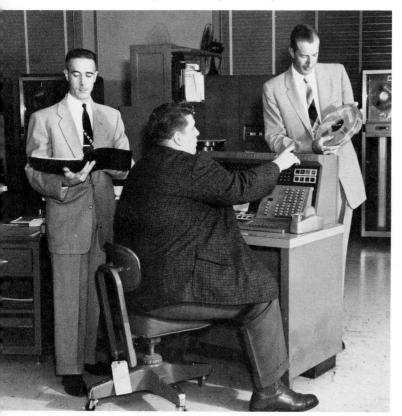

How new bills enter circulation: Left: Paper currency, printed and packaged by the Bureau of Engraving and Printing, is held in the United States treasurer's vault until needed. Right: One day's shipment from the treasurer to the nation's Federal Reserve banks in answer to requests from the banks for currency to meet expected demands.

The Bureau of Government Financial Operations occupies the Treasury annex, located across the street from the main Treasury building.

Form 1040.

INCOME TAX.

List No. ....

THE PENALTY

File No. ....

.... District of ....

FOR FAILURE TO HAVE THIS RETURN IN THE HANDS OF THE COLLECTOR OF INTERNAL REVENUE ON OR BEFORE MARCH 1 IS $20 TO $1,000.

Assessment List ....

Date received ....

(SEE INSTRUCTIONS ON PAGE 4.)

Page .... Line ....

UNITED STATES INTERNAL REVENUE.

RETURN OF ANNUAL NET INCOME OF INDIVIDUALS.

(As provided by Act of Congress, approved October 3, 1913.)

RETURN OF NET INCOME RECEIVED OR ACCRUED DURING THE YEAR ENDED DECEMBER 31, 191....

(FOR THE YEAR 1913, FROM MARCH 1, TO DECEMBER 31.)

Filed by (or for) .... of ....
(Full name of individual.)   (Street and No.)

In the City, Town, or Post Office of .... State of ....
(Fill in pages 2 and 3 before making entries below.)

1. GROSS INCOME (see page 2, line 12) .... $

2. GENERAL DEDUCTIONS (see page 3, line 7) .... $

3. NET INCOME .... $

Deductions and exemptions allowed in computing income subject to the normal tax of 1 per cent.

4. Dividends and net earnings received or accrued, of corporations, etc., subject to like tax. (See page 2, line 11) .... $

5. Amount of income on which the normal tax has been deducted and withheld at the source. (See page 2, line 9, column A) ....

6. Specific exemption of $3,000 or $4,000, as the case may be. (See Instructions 3 and 19) ....

Total deductions and exemptions. (Items 4, 5, and 6) .... $

7. TAXABLE INCOME on which the normal tax of 1 per cent is to be calculated. (See Instruction 3) . $

8. When the net income shown above on line 3 exceeds $20,000, the additional tax thereon must be calculated as per schedule below:

	INCOME.	TAX.
1 per cent on amount over $20,000 and not exceeding $50,000.... $		$
2 " " 50,000 " " 75,000....		
3 " " 75,000 " " 100,000....		
4 " " 100,000 " " 250,000....		
5 " " 250,000 " " 500,000....		
6 " " 500,000....		
Total additional or super tax .... $		
Total normal tax (1 per cent of amount entered on line 7).... $		
Total tax liability.... .... $		

The Nation's Tax Collector:
The Internal Revenue Service

Taxes have existed since the beginning of organized government. Every country has had to levy taxes and establish some sort of machinery for their collection. In 1789 the new United States government was no exception. When Alexander Hamilton became secretary of the treasury, he gave top priority to raising revenue, proposing that a duty be levied on all goods imported into the country and, in addition, an excise tax on wines and spirits. According to Hamilton, sound policy required that the duties and excises be "as high as will be consistent with the practicability of a safe collection."

At first, Congress thought otherwise in the case of excise taxes, partly out of fear of creating a large force of federal tax collectors who would "range the country prying into every man's house and affairs," as one congressman put it. But Hamilton persevered and in 1791 Congress, in its first important tax legislation, voted to tax a number of goods and services, including snuff, tobacco, carriages, auction sales, stamps, law-practice licenses, and spirits.

Along with imposing the taxes, Congress set up a system for collecting them under the supervision of

The first Form 1040 for reporting income for tax purposes. Issued in 1913 after the ratification of the Sixteenth Amendment and the passing of income tax legislation, Form 1040 became the best known of all government forms.

an assistant to the secretary of the treasury. The country was divided into fourteen districts, corresponding generally with state lines, in each of which there was a tax supervisor. The districts were further subdivided into inspection surveys, with as many inspectors in each as was deemed necessary. Since taxes were to be paid before the articles taxed were removed from the place where they were produced, each inspector was assigned to one or more locations. In the case of distilled spirits, the inspector marked and branded each cask with the name of the manufacturer and the quantity of spirits it contained. This was intended to prevent the reuse of the containers and the sale of spirits without payment of the tax.

Although the country needed the revenue, the new taxes proved unpopular with Americans who still remenbered how Britain had taxed the colonies. In various parts of the country irate citizens held protest meetings and at least one tax collector was tarred and feathered. The most serious of the protests was the Pennsylvania Whiskey Rebellion of 1794.

Tax legislation enacted in 1792 provided for a commissioner of the revenue, who, at a salary of $1,900 a year, was to be responsible for collecting all revenues except import and tonnage duties. The first incumbent, Tench Coxe of Pennsylvania, held several other posts as well, with the result that revenue collection was by no means his major concern.

The second commissioner of the revenue, William Miller, devoted more time to tax matters because he had to administer the Act of Assessment of 1798, which authorized the assessing of land and dwellings and the enumeration of slaves. After assessments had been made in each district, taxes were computed and tax bills delivered by the assessors.

In 1801 Congress, acting at the request of President Jefferson, abolished all excise taxes. Customs duties and the sale of public lands seemed to be capable of producing sufficient revenue. No money was needed for internal improvements, politicians of that day being agreed that this was not a province of the federal government. Moreover, a steady reduction of the public debt had improved the nation's credit.

During the summer of 1813, however, with a war with Britain in progress, a special session of Congress received a message from President James Madison appealing for additional funds. The President's message was accompanied by suggestions for tax legislation from Secretary of the Treasury Albert Gallatin. According to Gallatin, his proposals included only taxes already proved by experience, and even these were labeled temporary war measures to be in force for no more than one year after the cessation of hostilities. Congress gave Gallatin his taxes and also approved a $3 million direct tax to be collected by the states. To administer the new tax laws, Congress set up a collection agency and revived the office of commissioner of the revenue to run it. This time there were eighteen states to be divided into 191 internal revenue collection districts, each with a collector and a principal assessor. The districts were further subdivided into divisions and each collector was authorized to appoint as many deputies "as he may think proper." Congress made no provision for paying the deputies.

The Internal Revenue Service's National Office is located in this building at 1111 Constitution Avenue N.W. in the District of Columbia's Federal Triangle.

JAMES MADISON, *President of the United States of America,*

TO ALL WHO SHALL SEE THESE PRESENTS, GREETING:

𝕶𝖓𝖔𝖜 𝖄𝖊, That reposing special trust and confidence in the Integrity, Diligence and Discretion of *John Hoff,* *of Pennsylvania* I DO APPOINT him *PRINCIPAL ASSESSOR* under the act, entitled " An act for the assessment and collection of Direct Taxes and Internal duties," passed on the 22d day of July 1813, and the act, entitled " An act making further provision for the collection of Internal duties, and for the appointment and compensation of Assessors," passed on the 2d day of August, 1813, for the *Sixth* district in the state of *Pennsylvania* as designated in the first mentioned act; and do authorize and empower him to execute and fulfil the duties of that office according to law; *And to have and to hold* the said office, with all the rights and emoluments thereunto legally appertaining, unto him the said *John Hoff* during the pleasure of the President of the United States for the time being, and until the end of the next session of the Senate of the United States, and no longer.

IN TESTIMONY WHEREOF, I have caused these Letters to be made Patent, and the Seal of the United States to be hereunto affixed. GIVEN *under my hand, at the city of Washington, the Twenty Second day of November — in the year of our Lord one thousand eight hundred and Thirteen - and of the Independence of the United States of America, the thirty Eighth*

BY THE PRESIDENT,

James Madison

STATEMENT OF THE AMOUNTS

OF INTERNAL DUTIES,

Imposed by the United States, (except those on Stamps,) paid by each person in the first Collection District of Kentucky, during the year 1819.

	Bro! Forward $43.33
Moses Adams, ... $ 13.37	Spencer Adkin, ... $ 15.00
Caleb Asberry, ... 142.92	William Davis, ... 34.00
David Finley, ... 138.70	James French, ... 26.37
William Galt, ... 173.15	William Huckley, ... 441.82
Daniel Harrah, ... 79.00	Michael Hedrick, ... 248.78
William Johnson, ... 2.92	Matthew M'Clure, ... 79.70
Eli Metcalfe, ... 156.08	William Martin, ... 4.50
Thomas Pickett, (for a person unknown,) } 20.00	Joseph Power, ... 34.36
	Edmund Ragland, ... 73.32
Oliver Saunders, ... 50.27	John Snider, ... 18.25
Cornelius Summers, . . . 66.92	$ 1319.13
$843.33	

I certify that the foregoing statement exhibits the full amounts of the duties aforesaid, paid in the first collection district of Kentucky, during the year 1819.

GEO. W. BOTTS,

Collector of the Revenue for the first Collection District of Kentucky

September 30, 1819.

Flemingsburg—Printed at the STAR Office.

THE EVENING STAR.

WASHINGTON CITY:

THURSDAY................. JULY 3, 1862.

☞ *Reading matter on every page. See outside for interesting Telegraphic and other matter.*

☞ The President has approved and signed the following important bills:

The bill to aid in the construction of a railroad and telegraph line from the Missouri river to the Pacific ocean, and to secure the use of the same to the Government for postal, military, and other purposes.

The bill to provide internal revenue to defray the expenses of the Government and pay interest on the public debt.

The bill to prevent and punish the practice of polygamy in the Territories of the United States, and other places; and disapproving and annulling certain acts of the Legislative Assembly of the Territory of Utah.

The bill to prescribe an oath of office, and for other purposes.

FINANCIAL.—New York papers of last evening say: Stocks took a strong downward surge to-day. The continued silence of the Government in regard to affairs before Richmond produces an uncomfortable feeling, which is further increased by the call for three hundred thousand troops. The market would rally very quickly upon the slightest good news from Washington, and this may come at any moment. Prices seem to be controlled almost entirely by news from the seat of war.

Two early-nineteenth-century tax-related documents. Top: The letters patent, signed by President James Madison in 1813, appointing one John Hoff principal assessor for Pennsylvania's sixth district. Bottom: A statement issued in 1819 by the collector of revenue for the first collection district of Kentucky listing taxpayers and the amounts that they paid.

On July 3, 1862, the Washington Star *reported that President Lincoln had signed four important bills. The bill that resulted in the creation of the Office of Internal Revenue is the second one on the list.*

George S. Boutwell, who became the first commissioner of internal revenue in July 1862.

Reproduced here, a contemporary drawing showing citizens paying the first income tax in 1862.

Although the new taxes raised over $10 million, as much as 90 percent of the cost of the War of 1812 had to be met by borrowing. With the coming of peace, the tax laws were repealed, one by one, with the exception of some of the excise taxes. They were retained until 1817 in order to reduce the national debt, which amounted to $127 million. Once again the office of commissioner of the revenue was abolished, but customs duties, supplemented by proceeds from the sale of public lands, were sufficient to support the country's peacetime expenditures. In fact, during some of the years preceding the Civil War the federal government showed a budget surplus and ways had to be found to redistribute the extra funds.

All that changed when the Civil War began. At first plans were made to finance the conflict with borrowed money, but it soon became evident that additional revenue would be needed. A special session of Congress, meeting in Washington during the summer of 1861 to enact wartime legislation, gave quick approval to Secretary of the Treasury Salmon P. Chase's proposals for tax legislation. One bill called for a $20 million direct tax on real property to be apportioned among the states, free and slave alike. However, nobody had any illusions about collecting the taxes in the South. Another bill taxed incomes for the first time; the rate was set at 3 percent on incomes over $800.

(46.)

CLAIM UNDER SERIES 6, No. 14, FOR TAXES IMPROPERLY PAID

~~State~~ of *District of Columbia*, } ss:

~~County of~~

David Davis

of the * *City* of *Washington*, and State and county aforesaid, being duly *sworn* according to law, deposes and says, that † *he is the administrator of the estate of Abraham Lincoln deceased and that he is informed* ~~that he was~~ engaged in the business of *and believes* ‡ that upon the *fifteenth* day of *December*, A. D. 18*64*, *said Abraham Lincoln* was assessed by *P. M. Pearson*, Assessor of the District of said ~~State~~, *United* an internal revenue tax of *Twelve Hundred & Seventy nine 15/100* dollars, *Special income tax levied under Joint Resolution approved July 4. 1864* which amount he afterwards, on the *fifteenth* day of *December*, A. D. 18*64*, paid to * *Lewis Clephane*, Esq., Collector of Internal Revenue for the said district; which assessment and payment of the aforesaid tax was, as this deponent verily believes, erroneous and improper, for the following reasons, viz: *that as he is informed & believes that said assessment included a tax on his salary as President of the United States for the year ending December 31th 1863. which salary was ninety five thousand dollars —*

And this deponent now claims that, by reason of the aforesaid erroneous assessment and payment of the said sum of *Twelve hundred and Seventy nine 15/100* dollars, he *is* justly entitled to have the sum of *Twelve Hundred and fifty 2* dollars refunded, and *he* now ask *s* and demand *s* the same *debtor to the estate of said Abraham Lincoln* And this deponent further makes oath that he has not heretofore presented any claim for the refunding of the above amount, or any part thereof. ‖

David Davis

Sworn and subscribed before me, this *Twenty fifth*
day of *April*, A. D. 18*72.*

A. W. Middleton
Clerk Sup: Court U. S.

1.250 ⁷⁸
2.160 ¹⁶
141 ¹⁵
5355 94

* Here give Post Office address.
† If a member of a firm, state the fact here.
‡ Here state for or upon what the tax was assessed.
‖ If a claim has been presented before, state the fact in lieu of this.

K–1

Like countless well-meaning taxpayers who came after him, President Lincoln made a mistake in figuring his income tax. After the president's death, his estate contended that he had overpaid his 1864 tax by $1,279.15. The claim for taxes improperly paid is reproduced here.

A commissioner of taxes headed the Civil War tax collection apparatus. Each state and territory was assigned a principal collector and principal assessor, and each tax district had a collector and an assessor who were paid on a commission basis, a system which led to less than equitable treatment for some taxpayers.

As the winter of 1861 dragged on into the spring of 1862, the magnitude of the war began to be appreciated. Tax measures enacted in the special session of the previous summer no longer seemed adequate because of the sharp decline in customs revenues, while the income tax was not yet in operation. Moreover, the public debt was increasing at the rate of $2 million a day.

Congress responded to the emergency by passing the Internal Revenue Act of 1862, broad legislation that taxed incomes over $600, public utilities, occupations, spirits, tobacco, banks, insurance companies, and advertisements, and placed stamp taxes on certain commercial papers, medicines, perfumes, cosmetics, and playing cards. Numerous miscellaneous taxes extended even to persons who slaughtered hogs.

For such a far-reaching tax system, Congress created an entirely new collection organization under the direction of a commissioner of internal revenue, who had the power to assess, levy, and collect the taxes. George S. Boutwell, the first commissioner, entered upon his duties on July 17, 1862, and the office has been in continuous existence ever since.

In 1864 tax burdens increased when an Internal Revenue Act taxed a number of businesses by means of licenses and levied a 5 percent tax on incomes between $600 and $5,000 and a tax of up to 10 percent on income above $6,000.

As was to be expected, many citizens considered their wartime taxes to be excessive. When the Civil War finally ended and the costs of the military establishment began to fall, the public clamor for a tax reduction could not be ignored. The result was the dismantling of the wartime tax system, piece by piece. Americans were not to see anything quite like it again until near the end of World War 1 when the tax per capita approached $8.49, the level it had reached in 1866. The Internal Revenue Bureau managed to survive, however. In fact, the legislation that eliminated many of the wartime levies also defined in more detail the duties of the Commissioner of Internal Revenue and the organization of the bureau.

Between 1868 and 1913 nearly 90 percent of all United States internal revenue came from taxes on tobacco, distilled spirits, and fermented liquors. Nevertheless, these years were by no means a period of inactivity for the Bureau of Internal Revenue. It acquired a division to handle investigation and enforcement activities and, with the enactment of a tax on oleomargarine in 1886, an Analytical and Chemical Division, which determined the purity of the butter substitute by chemical analysis. And at various times, the bureau performed duties unrelated to the internal revenue system, as it did during the 1890s, for example, when Congress passed a law requiring all Chinese laborers in the United States to apply to the collector of revenue in their districts for a certificate of residence.

In 1894 a growing need for funds to operate the federal government led to the revival of the income tax. That year the Bureau of Internal Revenue established an Income Tax Division. The Supreme Court found the tax to be unconstitutional, however, a ruling that led, in 1913, to a constitutional amendment giving Congress the power to "lay and collect taxes on incomes, from whatever source derived, without apportionment among the several states, and without regard to any census or enumeration." Legislation, enacted in 1913, imposing taxes on the net incomes of both individuals and corporations ushered in a period of great expansion for the Bureau of Internal Revenue. During the next fiscal year alone, tax receipts increased by $40 million, a large sum in those days.

During the months before the country entered World War 1 the United States was fortunate to have an income tax system already in operation as government expenditures increased while imports from Europe, and duties collected on imports, decreased three and one-half times over the preceding rates went up as did excise taxes on spirits, tobacco, and other products. The augmented taxes, along with new levies, placed an added burden on the Bureau of Internal Revenue. To meet it, the bureau underwent a reorganization in 1917. At the same time more employees were hired to handle the added volume of collections, which in fiscal year 1918 increased three and one half times over the preceding

APR 27 1872

United States Internal Revenue,
Assessor's Office, District of Columbia.

Washington, *April 27th* 1872.

I hereby certify that Abraham Lincoln made two returns of income for the year ending, Dec. 31. 1863, one for his tax on income outside of his salary, amounting to $7.75 being a tax of 1½ d. on $1183; the second was for the tax as levied by the joint resolution of July 4. 1864, and known as the Special income tax, which embraces the above amount and his salary of $25.000 as President of the United States, amounting in the aggregate to $25.583 on which he paid tax of 5 d. amount of tax $1279.15 Both of these returns appear on Form 58 for Dec. 1864, and are the only returns he made to this office.

Walter S. Burr.
Assessor

Supporting documents in the Lincoln tax claim.

ASSISTANT ASSESSOR'S CERTIFICATE.

I hereby certify that I have carefully investigated the facts set forth in the within affidavit, and that I believe the statements to be in all respects just and true. *S. L. Clements*

Dated *April 26th* 187*2*.   Division.   District.   Assistant Assessor,

ASSESSOR'S CERTIFICATE.

I hereby certify that I have carefully investigated the facts set forth in the within affidavit of *David Davis, administrator*, and that I believe the statements to be in all respects just and true; and I further certify, that from present personal examination I find the sum of *Twelve hundred & Seventy nine* dollars and *fifteen* cents reported against the said *Abraham Lincoln* on page *6*, line *6*, of the list on form *58* for *December*, 1864; also the sum of ——— dollars and ——— cents, reported against ——— on page ———, line ——— of the list on form ——— for ———, 18—. now on file in my office; and that the tax is included in the Collector's aggregate receipt for the said list transmitted by me to the Commissioner of Internal Revenue; and that the claim has not heretofore been allowed in any form. Said receipt amounts to $ *16.880.44*

Walter S. Burr

Dated *April 26th* 1872.   *for*   District, *Columbia*   Assessor,

COLLECTOR'S CERTIFICATE.

I hereby certify that I have carefully investigated the facts set forth in the within affidavit, and am satisfied that the statements are in all respects just and true; and I further certify, upon personal examination, that I find the sum of *Twelve hundred & Seventy one* dollars and *Fifteen* cents reported against the said *Abraham Lincoln* on page *8* line *18*, of the list ——— of ——— dollars and ——— cents reported against ——— on page ——— line ——— of the list on form ——— for ——— 18— now on file in my office; and that the same was paid to me on the *15th* day of *December*, 18*64* and on the ——— day of ———, 18—, and are included in his aggregate receipts for said lists, the receipts amounting to $ *16.880.44* and $ ———, respectively, and delivered to the Assessor, to be transmitted to the Commissioner of Internal Revenue; and that no claim for the assessment herein complained of has heretofore been presented.*

Thos. L. Tullock

Dated *June 26th* 1872.   *for the*   District, of *Columbia*   Collector,

Between 1878 and 1959 this tax-paid stamp featuring the likeness of De Witt Clinton appeared on more than 490 billion packs of cigarettes.

In this turn-of-the-century photo, clerks are packing Internal Revenue stamps for shipment to manufacturers of taxed products.

year. For the first time the federal government collected taxes in excess of the billion dollar mark — the exact figure was $3,698,955,821.

"Fiscal year 1918 marks the beginning of a new era of internal revenue taxation," noted Commissioner of Internal Revenue Daniel C. Roper in his annual report for that year. And he observed: "The nature of the change . . . is not merely a transference of the tax burden from one to another set of objects, but rather a transformation from a system of heterogeneous taxation based on expediency to a system of taxation comprehensive in scope and conforming consistently to a new and essentially different economic theory."

The federal revenue system was indeed undergoing a substantial change. For some time prior to the First World War excise and custom levies had been increasingly less productive. But the adoption of the 16th Amendment in 1913 provided a new source of revenue which, in large part, made up for the loss of income from the old taxes. The Revenue Act of 1918 set the seal on the new era. The act changed the rates for many taxes; however, its real import lay in its codification of the then-existing tax laws. The legislation repealed earlier laws and brought within the bounds of a single law all provisions relating to income, profits, and excise taxes. It was at this time that the bureau set up its Intelligence Division to detect and bring to justice those guilty of tax frauds against the government.

Collections by the Bureau of Internal Revenue reached an all time high in 1920—$5.4 billion—not to be equaled again until 1938. In 1920 the number of bureau employees passed the fifteen thousand mark, more than triple the figure for 1917.

This photo was taken in the Treasury building cafeteria when the Revenue Service's Training School graduated its first class of special agents. A cake at the lower right is inscribed: "First Special Agents School Graduation, Washington, D.C., April 29, 1960."

By 1922 bureau employees numbered almost eighteen thousand. The federal revenue system had grown as it changed.

Declining expenditures and budget surpluses marked the postwar years; the repeal of some taxes and the lowering of others did not substantially alter the situation. It was at this time that the Bureau of Internal Revenue began to make extensive use of machines in duplicating tax records. The bureau also set up branch offices throughout the country to make the tax collector more accessible to the taxpayer.

In 1919, following the ratification of the 18th Amendment and the passing of the Volstead Prohibition Enforcement Act, the Bureau of Internal Revenue established its celebrated Prohibition Unit, a forerunner of the Treasury's Bureau of Alcohol, Tobacco and Firearms. The Volstead Act specifically charged the commissioner of internal revenue with primary responsibility for investigation and enforcement of the prohibitory terms of the amendment. Prosecution in the courts was to be conducted by the Department of Justice. One branch of the new Prohibition Unit was responsible for the enforcement of the penal and regulatory provisions of the act, while a second branch supervised the administrative features of the law covering traffic in nonbeverage alcohol. The act gave to the commissioner of internal revenue authority to issue permits for the manufacture and sale of spirits for religious, industrial, and medicinal purposes. Any such products were subject to existing excise taxes and the commissioner was empowered to collect them.

During fiscal year 1925, a busy twelve months for the Prohibition Unit, over 3,700 Bureau of Internal Revenue employees were engaged in drug and prohibition enforcement alone. They made more than 77,000 arrests of prohibition-law violators, in some cases with the cooperation of state law enforcement officers. The appraised value of seized property totaled $11,200,00. Thirty-nine bureau agents were injured and seven were killed in the performance of their duties.

The work of the Prohibition Unit continued until 1927 when a Federal Prohibition Bureau with primary enforcement responsibility was organized in the Department of Justice. However, in 1933, after ratification of the 21st Amendment to the Constitution, which repealed the 18th Amendment and permitted legal manufacture and sale of alcohol, enforcement of federal liquor laws returned to the Internal Revenue Bureau along with regulatory and tax collecting responsibilities. Today, the Treasury's Bureau of Alcohol, Tobacco and Firearms administers and enforces revenue laws affecting industrial alcohol, distilled spirits, wine, and beer.

When the depression of 1929 descended upon the country, an era of budget surpluses came to an end. Revenue fell off as the nation's income decreased. In 1932 revenue collections, amounting to just over $1.5 billion, were lower than at any time since 1917. Moreover, the cost of collecting each $100 was higher than at any time since 1898.

In spite of the decrease in revenue, there was tremendous pressure on the federal government to do something about the large numbers of unemployed. In 1932 Congress passed legislation authorizing loans to the states for relief purposes. Other legislation, aimed at relieving the problems of the unemployed and reviving the economy, followed. Such programs required large appropriations, and Congress raised income tax rates and lowered the exemption level. The rates of existing estate taxes were more than doubled, gift taxes were reenacted, and numerous other levies were authorized. In ensuing years Congress approved additional programs for relief and for economic stimulation, sharply increasing government expenditures.

The Bureau of Internal Revenue organized new divisions and units to administer the tax aspects of the legislative programs enacted by Congress, including a Processing Tax Division to collect the taxes levied under the Agricultural Adjustment Act of 1933 and related legislation. By 1935 these taxes were responsible for well over a half billion dollars of revenue. A year later, however, the Agricultural Adjustment Act was challenged in the courts and found to be an improper exercise of federal taxing power. Congress then passed legislation to allow the refund of taxes collected under the act.

Other legislation also required special administrative and collection machinery. For instance, the Silver Tax Division was organized in 1934 to administer the Silver Purchase Act of that year, which provided for the imposition of a tax equal to 50 percent of the net profit realized on the transfer of ownership of silver bullion. A Sales Tax Division was set

To mark its hundredth anniversary in 1962 the Internal Revenue Service issued the documentary stamp reproduced here. Intended for use on bonds, deeds, debentures, and other legal documents, the stamp carries a picture of the Revenue Service's National Office.

Some of the Internal Revenue Service's modern data processing equipment can be seen in this photo taken at the National Computer Center at Martinsburg, West Virginia, where the service operates a centralized account system for all taxpayers.

A delinquent taxpayer confers with a Revenue Service officer to arrange for payment of overdue taxes. Tax officers try to set up payment plans that will not cause the taxpayer undue hardship.

A representative of the Revenue Service's Taxpayer Service Division offers advice on the correct preparation of a tax return.

A Service Center employee, working at what is called a "tingle table," opens mail and determines where it should go for processing.

At the Kansas City Service Center income tax returns are routed to the Examination Branch where they are checked for accuracy.

At the Revenue Service's Kansas City Service Center, one of ten such centers distributed about the country, an employee sorts incoming mail by internal revenue district and type of tax involved.

up to supervise the collection of manufacturers' excises, documentary stamp taxes, occupational taxes, and a number of miscellaneous taxes.

In 1937 the Internal Revenue Bureau put into operation its Social Security Tax Division to administer Social Security taxes. At that time employers of eight or more persons were taxed at a rate of 1 percent of wages paid; they withheld a similar tax for their employees. The Social Security Tax Division collected over $250 million in 1937.

Although the pressures of the depression began to disappear when the Second World War broke out, government expenditures continued to grow, especially after the United States entered the conflict. Taxes on incomes were increased sharply, corporate taxes were raised, and many existing excises were revised upward. In 1945 the Internal Revenue Bureau collected well over $43 billion, a record amount, and the tax per capita reached the figure of $312.13. In 1946 the total number of persons employed by the Bureau of Internal Revenue rose to a record 59,693.

Despite increased tax revenues, the government was forced to borrow heavily during World War II, and postwar defense spending experienced only a brief decline before the cold war and the Korean conflict forced expenditures up again. Although there were some reductions in rates and repeals of wartime levies, World War II collection figures were exceeded as the nation's production and employment burgeoned.

Increased activity brought a new look to the Internal Revenue Bureau. A reorganization program, inaugurated in 1952, overhauled the administration of the federal tax system. There was even a name change — to Internal Revenue Service. Politically appointed collectors were succeeded by directors hired under the Civil Service merit system, and the administration of tax laws was further decentralized, a trend that was to continue.

Today seven regional commissioners of internal revenue and the fifty-eight district offices and ten service centers for which they are responsible handle much of the business of the Internal Revenue Service. The regional headquarters are located in Cincinnati, Ohio (Central), Philadelphia, Pennsylvania (Mid-Atlantic), Chicago, Illinois (Midwest), New York City (North Atlantic), Atlanta, Georgia (Southeast), Dallas, Texas (Southwest), and San Francisco, California (Western).

In 1961 the Internal Revenue Service launched one of the most revolutionary programs in its history when it began a conversion to automatic data-

This employee is transferring information from tax returns to magnetic computer tape for the Internal Revenue Service's Integrated Data Retrieval System, which has greatly reduced the time needed to answer queries from taxpayers.

processing equipment to handle the more than 100 million tax returns and half a billion related documents that it receives each year from United States taxpayers. High-speed electronic equipment, installed in ten regional data-processing service centers distributed across the country and at the National Computer Center at Martinsburg, West Virginia, now handle the processing of returns in a centralized account system that includes all taxpayers. The system was designed to improve tax administration, ensure compliance with tax laws, and provide better service to taxpayers. To further these objectives, the Internal Revenue Service has established an Office of the Assistant Commissioner of Accounts Collection and Taxpayer Service and a Taxpayer Service Division.

Each year the Internal Revenue Service collects in excess of $300 billion from American taxpayers, with more than $200 billion of that sum coming from income and profits taxes. The service's organization and its collection procedures have changed considerably since Congress created the Office of the Commissioner of Internal Revenue in 1862, but its objective remains the same: to encourage and achieve the highest possible degree of voluntary compliance with tax laws and regulations and to maintain the highest degree of public confidence in the integrity of the service.

This gold display at the Old Mint was valued at $1 million.
The nuggets were on loan from Sierra County, California; the
gold bars were from United States stores held at the San Fran-
cisco Assay Office.

Small Change Is Big Business:
The Bureau of the Mint

PRODUCING THE MILLIONS OF COINS THAT Americans carry in their pockets for use when a small sum is called for is the function of the Treasury's Bureau of the Mint.

The mint of the United States began turning out coins in 1793 in Philadelphia, then the nation's capital. Since the War for Independence, Americans, lacking a coinage of their own, had continued to use English shillings, French louis d'or, Spanish dollars, and other coins that had circulated freely since colonial days. It was a confusing system, however, and one that slowed trade as buyers and sellers sought to agree on prices in terms of the coins being offered in payment.

Congress took the first step toward providing the United States with its own distinctive coinage in 1792 when it passed the Mint Act. In addition to authorizing a mint, the act called for a monetary system based on bimetallism, with silver and gold full legal tender at a ratio of 15 to 1. The decimal system was to be the method of reckoning and the dollar the unit of money.

The mint began its operations in Philadelphia under the supervision of the secretary of state, an arrangement favored by President George Washington, who took a deep interest in the affairs of the mint. In fact, Washington is said to have furnished some of his family silver to be melted down for the

mint's first coinage. The silver half dismes, or half dimes, of the first coinage did not go into circulation, but were presented to Martha Washington who gave them to her friends as souvenirs. In a message to Congress the president referred to that initial coinage as a "small beginning."

The mint's hand-operated press produced its first coins for regular circulation—11,178 one-cent pieces—in March 1793. Coinage of silver dollars commenced the next year and David Rittenhouse, the first director of the mint, reported to Congress: "A beginning has been made in coining the precious metals. . . . A large parcel of blank dollars is ready for coining, waiting for a more powerful press to be finished, in order to complete them for currency."

Between 1794 and 1805 the mint produced 1,439,517 silver dollars. Unfortunately, many of the dollars ended up in Mexico and the West Indies, leaving very few for circulation in the United States. Secretary of State James Madison discussed the problem in a letter to Director of the Mint Robert Patterson in 1806: "In consequence of a representation from the director of the Bank of the United States that considerable purchases have been made of dollars coined at the Mint for the purpose of exporting them, and as it is probable further purchases and exportations will be made, the President directs that all silver to be coined at the Mint shall be small denominations, so that the largest piece shall not exceed half a dollar."

No more silver dollars were minted until 1836, when a thousand were coined. The mint resumed production of silver dollars on a regular basis in 1839.

In addition to silver dollars, the Mint Act authorized the production of silver half dollars, quarter dollars, dimes, and half dimes. The mint also turned out gold coins called eagles, worth $10, gold half eagles and quarter eagles, and copper cents and half cents.

In 1799 the mint became an independent agency, reporting directly to the president, a status it retained until 1873 when, as the Bureau of the Mint, it became part of the Department of the Treasury. At that time coins were produced in Philadelphia and at branch mints in San Francisco, California, and Carson City, Nevada. Assay offices, where gold and silver bullion were bought and disbursed and paper money could be redeemed for specie, had been opened in New York City, Denver, Colorado, and Boise City, Idaho.

San Francisco's mint began operations in 1854 after the large amount of gold being mined in California proved too much for the Philadelphia mint to handle. Moreover, shipping gold across the country was both risky and time consuming. The mint at Carson City turned out coins from 1870 until 1893. It then became an assay office and closed permanently in 1933. Other early mints were located at Dahlonega, Georgia, in operation from 1838 until 1861, and at New Orleans, Louisiana, where coins were produced from 1838 until 1861

An oil painting by John Dunsmore in which the artist shows George and Martha Washington inspecting the first United States coins. David Rittenhouse, the newly appointed director of the mint, stands at Mrs. Washington's left.

and from 1879 until 1909. New Orleans also operated as an assay office from 1876 until 1942, when it was closed.

Today, United States mints are located in Philadelphia and Denver; the latter began coinage operations in 1906 after forty-four years as an assay office. In addition, the San Francisco Assay Office produces some coins.

In the years since 1793 there have been several changes in the denominations of the coins produced in the United States as well as changes in their content. Gold coins were withdrawn from circulation in 1933 and are no longer produced. Other coins no longer in use include the half-cent, two-cent, three-cent, and twenty-cent pieces, and the silver half dime, which was replaced by the five-cent nickel in 1866.

Coin designs change infrequently in the United States. By law, once a design has been adopted it cannot be changed for twenty-five years except by a special act of Congress. There is no limitation on the period beyond twenty-five years that a design may remain in use.

New coin designs do appear from time to time. On these occasions artists are asked to submit possible designs for the obverse, or face, of the coin and for the reverse. The director of the mint, with the approval of the secretary of the treasury, usually chooses the design to be used. In a few instances Congress has selected the design for a coin.

A small screw press similar to the one in this drawing produced the first coins struck by the United States Mint. By April 1795, larger presses were in operation and the original press may have been retired after turning out less than 300,000 coins, mostly cents and half cents.

LETTER

FROM

THE DIRECTOR OF THE MINT,

ACCOMPANYING

A REPORT,

And fundry Statements, numbered 1, 2, 3 and 4,

Made in Purfuance of a Refolution of the Houfe of the 18th Inftant.

December 19, 1797.

Printed by Order of the Houfe of Reprefentatives.

Philadelphia:

PRINTED BY JOSEPH GALES

No. 126, North Second Street.

When the Director of the Mint sent his report for 1797 to Congress, it carried the cover reproduced here.

Steam-powered presses had been installed at the Philadelphia Mint by 1836. The first model to be used is pictured here.

F.B. Schell made this drawing of an employee striking coins at the Philadelphia Mint, circa 1853. A group of sightseers has been included in the picture.

This Grecian-style building was the home of the Philadelphia Mint from 1832 until 1901.

The original United States Mint.

Today this modern building houses the Philadelphia Mint. Located on Independence Mall near the site of the first United States Mint, it has equipment designed to provide mechanized, continuous operations during the entire coinage process, from virgin metals to finished coins.

When this photo was taken, members of the USSR gymnastics team were visiting the Philadelphia Mint. The gymnasts are looking at a display of bicentennial coin and medal designs.

One of the Philadelphia Mint's information specialists (arrow) and a visiting elementary school class. The group is standing in front of the official display of medals produced by the United States Mint.

The United States Mint in Denver, Colorado. Most of the cents and nickels in circulation are produced in Denver.

For the Lincoln cent, issued in 1909 on the one hundredth anniversary of Lincoln's birth, only one artist was asked to submit a design. He was Victor David Brenner, recommended by President Theodore Roosevelt who greatly admired a plaque of Lincoln executed by the artist. Brenner's design with its bust of Lincoln on the obverse marked a radical de-

The historic Old Mint, located at San Francisco's Fifth and Mission streets. Coinage operations began in this building in 1874 when it replaced a smaller mint building. The Old Mint, a national historic landmark, has been returned to Treasury Department custody and renovated after some thirty years of use as an office building. It now houses the Bureau of the Mint's Data Center and Special Coinage and Medals Division and the Old Mint Museum.

parture from accepted styling. Previously in the United States portraits had not been used on coins of a regular series. The reverse of the Lincoln cent displayed two wheat heads in memorial style. Between them in the center of the coin are the words "ONE CENT" and "UNITED STATES OF AMERICA." "E PLURIBUS UNUM," a Latin motto meaning "out of many, one," appears at the top. A new reverse featuring the Lincoln Memorial was adopted in 1959.

Portraits of United States presidents now appear on all coins being manufactured: Thomas Jefferson on the five-cent piece, Franklin Roosevelt on the dime, George Washington on the quarter, John F. Kennedy on the half dollar, and Dwight D. Eisenhower on the dollar.

In honor of the nation's bicentennial the designs on the reverse of the quarter, half dollar, and dollar were changed in 1975. The reverse of the bicentennial quarter features a colonial drummer; the reverse of the half dollar depicts Philadelphia's Independence Hall; and the dollar reverse shows the Liberty Bell and the moon. The designs were chosen after a national competition. The obverse sides of the three coins remained the same except for a change in date to "1776—1976." The Bureau of the Mint announced that it planned to produce at least 1.6 billion of the bicentennial quarters, 550 million half dollars, and 300 million dollars for issue through 1976 after which the coins would again be minted with the date of coinage. They would continue to bear the bicentennial design on the reverse until the secretary of the treasury decided otherwise.

When a new design has been selected for a coin, Bureau of the Mint craftsmen prepare a plasticene model in bas-relief from the approved sketch. The model is from three to twelve times larger than the finished coin and is used to make a plaster of Paris negative. A plaster positive made from the negative is submitted for approval before the several steps that lead to the production of working dies are undertaken. Once the working dies are ready, coin manufacture can begin.

In addition to its regular coin production, the Bureau of the Mint turns out proof coins, flawless

Restored to its former appearance, the Superintendent's Office is a popular attraction at the Old Mint Museum.

coins with a mirrorlike finish that are specially sealed and packaged for numismatists. In its early days the mint produced limited numbers of high quality coins called specimen, or master, coins for presentation to foreign governments, visiting dignitaries, and important Americans. Public sale of proof coins began in 1858. The Philadelphia mint manufactured the coins until 1964 when the press of other business caused the program to be suspended. In 1968 production of proof coins was resumed at the United States Assay Office in San Francisco.

Proof coins are made from carefully selected, scratch-free blanks that have been given a high polish. The dies used in the stamping process are also highly polished and they are used only for proof coins. Each coin is struck twice to produce a very sharp relief and carefully checked for defects that might have occurred in the minting operation. Im-

perfect coins are melted; they are not placed in circulation.

Only coins currently manufactured for general circulation are produced as proof coins. Since they are of San Francisco mintage, they bear an "S" mark. The San Francisco Assay Office sells proof coins on a first-come, first-served basis.

Uncirculated coins are another mint product popular with collectors. The coins represent the very best that can be made with the techniques used in the regular coinage process. Like proof coins, uncirculated coins are sealed into special packages. They can be ordered by mail from the San Francisco Assay Office or purchased at one of the Bureau of the Mint's sales counters.

The Bureau of the Mint strikes a medallion honoring each new president of the United States. In all, the bureau has produced and has available for sale

In addition to its gold- and silver-refining operations, the New York Assay Office, pictured here, produces special coins for the Bureau of the Mint. The building is located on the East River waterfront.

The San Francisco Assay Office at Duboce and Hermann streets. Coinage operations were moved here from the Old Mint in 1937, discontinued in 1955, and resumed in 1965.

over three hundred medals in several series. In addition to the presidential series, there is a presidential miniature series, a national historical series, an army series, and a navy series, among others. The Bureau of the Mint also manufactures the medals that are presented as awards by the armed services.

Most of the monetary gold and silver stocks belonging to the United States are stored in depositories that are part of the Bureau of the Mint. Silver is stored at the Bullion Depository at West Point, New York, and gold at the Fort Knox Bullion Depository in Kentucky.

Silver held at the United States Bullion Depository at West Point is stored in a one-story concrete building surrounded by a nine-foot-high steel fence. Within the building a series of vault compartments can be reached only through a drill- and flame-proof door equipped with a time lock. Bullion trucks enter the depository building through a vertical-lift steel door, which then closes to provide security for loading operations.

Sentries in watchtowers keep the surrounding terrain under constant observation, and a gate controlled by guards regulates the movement of traffic into and out of the depository area, which adjoins the West Point military reservation.

Part of the New York Assay Office's electrolytic refinery. Several million fine troy ounces of silver are produced here each year.

A step in the coining process: reducing a strip of alloy to the desired thickness.

Located on the Fort Knox military reservation's Gold Vault Road, the Fort Knox Bullion Depository began operations in 1937. The depository occupies a two-story, basement, and attic building of granite, steel, and concrete. Inside is a two-level, compartmented steel and concrete vault, with a door that weighs more than twenty tons.

Most of the nation's gold bullion is stored in the Fort Knox vault in the form of standard mint bars of almost pure gold or coin gold bars made from melted gold coins. The bars, about the size of an ordinary building brick, weigh 27½ pounds each. Because they are stored without wrappings, the bars must be handled with great care to avoid abrasion of the soft metal.

As it is at the West Point Depository, security is very strict at Fort Knox. No one person is entrusted with the combination to the vault. Instead, several staff members must dial a portion of the combination known only to them. There is a trained guard force and the building is equipped with the latest protec-

tive devices. In addition, there are guard posts at each corner of the building and guards at the entrance gate. The depository has its own emergency power plant and water system.

The director of the mint, whose offices are in the Treasury building in Washington, supervises the Bureau of the Mint's numerous activities as they are carried out by the Philadelphia and Denver mints, the assay offices in New York City and San Francisco, and the bullion depositories at West Point and Fort Knox.

Finished coins are counted and bagged before being sent to Federal Reserve banks.

These leftover scraps from which blanks for one-cent pieces have been punched will be melted and used again.

The Jefferson five-cent piece, adopted in 1938.

Some Products of the Bureau of the Mint

The Roosevelt dime, introduced in 1946.

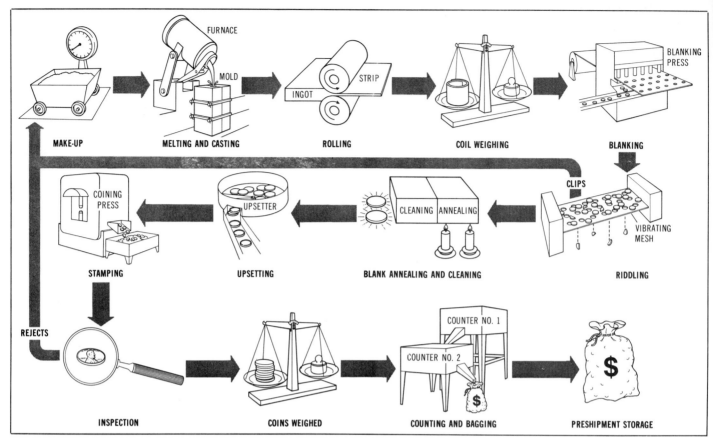

MAKE-UP MELTING AND CASTING ROLLING COIL WEIGHING BLANKING

FURNACE MOLD INGOT STRIP BLANKING PRESS

COINING PRESS UPSETTER CLEANING ANNEALING CLIPS VIBRATING MESH

STAMPING UPSETTING BLANK ANNEALING AND CLEANING RIDDLING

REJECTS INSPECTION COINS WEIGHED COUNTER NO. 1 COUNTER NO. 2 COUNTING AND BAGGING PRESHIPMENT STORAGE

How coins are made: pennies and nickels.

The quarter dollar, introduced in 1932 to commemorate the two-hundredth anniversary of first President George Washington's birth.

164

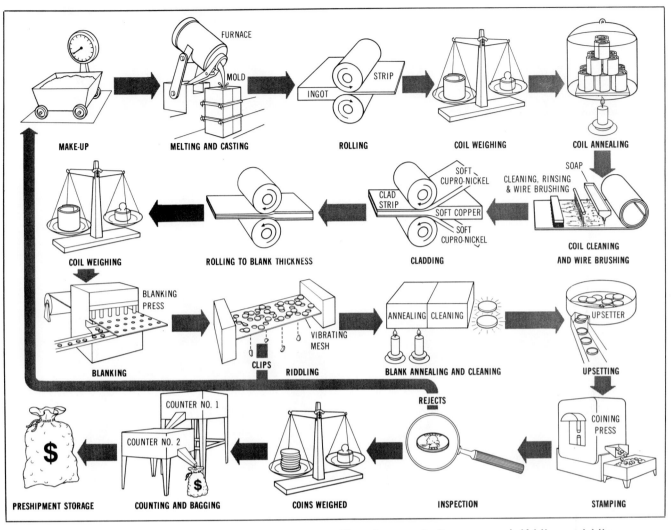

FURNACE
MOLD
INGOT STRIP
SOAP
CLEANING, RINSING
& WIRE BRUSHING

MAKE-UP   MELTING AND CASTING   ROLLING   COIL WEIGHING   COIL ANNEALING

SOFT CUPRO-NICKEL
CLAD STRIP
SOFT COPPER
SOFT CUPRO-NICKEL

COIL WEIGHING   ROLLING TO BLANK THICKNESS   CLADDING   COIL CLEANING AND WIRE BRUSHING

BLANKING PRESS
VIBRATING MESH
ANNEALING   CLEANING
UPSETTER

BLANKING   CLIPS   RIDDLING   BLANK ANNEALING AND CLEANING   UPSETTING

COUNTER NO. 1
COUNTER NO. 2
REJECTS
COINING PRESS

PRESHIPMENT STORAGE   COUNTING AND BAGGING   COINS WEIGHED   INSPECTION   STAMPING

How coins are made: dimes, quarters, half dollars, and dollars.

The Kennedy half dollar, issued in 1964 as a tribute to the assassinated president.

Left to right: *The bicentennial quarter dollar, half dollar, and dollar issued by the Bureau of the Mint in honor of the nation's two-hundredth anniversary celebration with a new patriotic design on the reverse and a change in date, "1776–1976," on the obverse.*

The John Adams medal in the mint's presidential series. The design on the reverse indicates that the medal was intended for presentation to Indian chiefs as a token of friendship. Medals in the presidential series measure three inches in diameter.

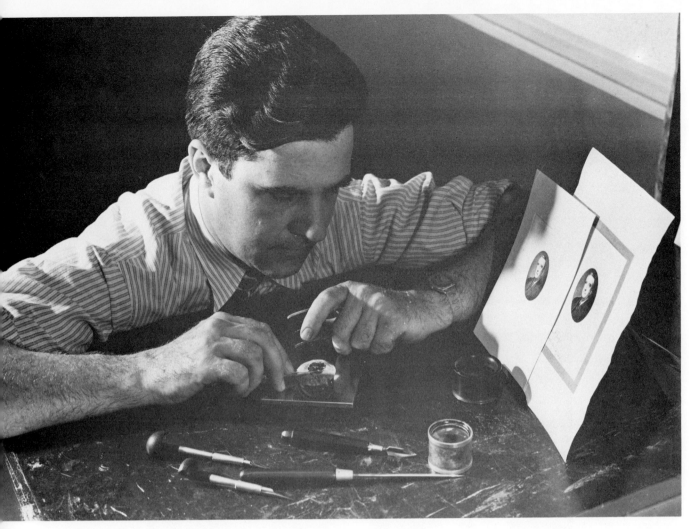

A skilled engraver works on a steel die for one of the medals issued by the Bureau of the Mint.

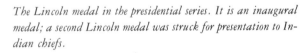

The Lincoln medal in the presidential series. It is an inaugural medal; a second Lincoln medal was struck for presentation to Indian chiefs.

The Albert Gallatin medal in the mint's secretaries of the Treasury series. It carries the Treasury seal on the reverse.

The portrait on Gerald R. Ford's official medal was executed by Frank Gasparro, the mint's chief sculptor and engraver. The reverse is the work of mint engraver Matthew Pelso.

This is the Andrew Jackson medal in the mint's United States Army series. On the reverse, "Battle of New Orleans, January 8, 1815," is inscribed below the representation of the Winged Victory.

Since 1938 this fortress-like building at West Point, New York, has served as the Treasury's silver bullion depository.

The United States Bullion Depository at Fort Knox, Kentucky, where most of the nation's gold stocks are stored.

Director of the Mint Mary T. Brooks in Compartment 33 of the gold vault at the Fort Knox Bullion Depository. Mrs. Brooks was director of the mint from 1969 until 1977. When the photo was taken, Compartment 33 contained gold bars valued at $499,823,244.58.

BUY WAR BONDS

Selling Bonds: The United States Savings Bonds Division

ITS SAVINGS BONDS DIVISION WAS ORGANIZED ONLY in 1946, but the United States Treasury has sold bonds to individual citizens since the earliest days of the country. Proceeds from the sale of bonds have been used to finance wars, to acquire territories, and to build railroads and canals.

Bonds played an important role in the financing of the Civil War. While raising money to pay for that conflict, Treasury officials learned that house-to-house selling and person-to-person contacts increased bond sales. During the Spanish-American War small denomination bonds found a ready market, with more than a quarter million people subscribing to issues that ranged in value from $20 to $300. The Treasury profited from its bond-selling experience during World War I when it staged four Liberty Loan campaigns and one postwar Victory Loan drive, raising a total of $21,435,370,600 for the war effort. The highly successful Fourth Liberty Loan raised nearly $7 billion from 22 million subscribers, more than one-fifth the total population of the United States at that time.

World War I bonds were marketable securities, but if they had to be sold before maturity, it was often at a substantial discount. Sometimes sellers received as little as 82¢ on the dollar. Consequently, when the Treasury reentered the small denomination bond market in 1935, it offered a different type of bond. Popularly called "baby bonds," the Treasury's new bonds had fixed redemption values and they were redeemable at any time after a short initial holding period. Moreover, the Treasury registered the name of the bond purchaser along with the identification number of his bond. If the bond was lost or destroyed, it could be replaced. The bonds were issued in $25 to $1,000 denominations and sold at 75 percent of their face value. They paid 2.9 percent interest if held to their full ten-year maturity. The United States Treasurer's Office and fourteen thousand post offices distributed throughout the country handled bond sales, which were promoted by direct mail and magazine advertising.

Baby bonds were introduced to encourage public participation in government financing and they were the Treasury's first real savings bonds. The sales campaign began with the purchase of a bond by President Franklin Delano Roosevelt at a White House ceremony on March 1, 1935, and during the next five years some 2 million investors bought 11 million bonds; their purchases represented $3 billion in maturity value.

In 1941, with a war raging in Europe, the United States was increasing its defense expenditures. To raise money and to cool a serious threat of inflation, the Treasury decided to expand its savings bond program. Baby bonds, which had been issued in four

172

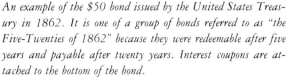

An example of the $50 bond issued by the United States Treasury in 1862. It is one of a group of bonds referred to as "the Five-Twenties of 1862" because they were redeemable after five years and payable after twenty years. Interest coupons are attached to the bottom of the bond.

As an economy measure, the backs of Civil War bonds were not engraved. The typographically produced back of a $100 bond is seen here.

successive series, A, B, C, and D, were replaced by the series E defense bond, and again President Roosevelt made the first purchase. Like the baby bonds, the series E bonds were sold at 75 percent of face value and paid 2.9 percent interest if held to their ten-year maturity. The 2.9 percent was an average figure, the actual rate of return being smaller during the early part of the ten-year period and greater as a bond approached maturity. A purchaser could redeem his bond after holding it for two months, but the bonds could not be sold or transferred, except back to the Treasury.

Defense bonds were offered in $25, $50, $100, and $1,000 denominations, and they were available only to individual buyers who were limited to purchases totaling no more than $5,000 in maturity value in any one year. The bonds were sold at banks and, in the beginning, at some post offices.

After the United States became an active participant in the war, the Treasury changed the name of its series E bond to series E war savings bond and

Treasury employees assigned to the bond program became the War Savings Staff.

Meanwhile, the Treasury sought to expand its bond sales through the use of volunteers. Volunteers had been a major factor in the success of the World War I Liberty Loans and they proved to be equally valuable during World War II. The nation's banks acted as voluntary sales agents; community leaders organized volunteer bond sales committees; and volunteers from the advertising and communications industries encouraged the public to buy bonds, stressing both the nation's need for funds and the citizen's opportunity to make a good investment.

Another successful World War I program to be revived was the use of savings stamps to supplement and encourage bond sales. The Treasury issued the stamps, which carried a reproduction of David Chester French's famous statue The Minute Man, in 10¢, 25¢, 50¢, $1, and $5 denominations. When a buyer had accumulated $18.75 worth of stamps, he exchanged them for a $25 series E bond. The Treasury

In this 1919 photo Secretary of the Treasury Carter Glass displays the first Victory Loan bond to come off the printing press at the Bureau of Engraving and Printing.

supplied stamp booklets to encourage children to save "a dime at a time," usually on weekly stamp sale days at school. Although stamp sales were not limited to students, an estimated 25 million of them bought stamps.

Young people sold as well as bought stamps. Newspaper carriers, who participated in a program initiated in the fall of 1941 by the *Philadelphia Evening Bulletin*, proved to be excellent stamp salesmen. Some 150,000 carriers, representing 900 different newspapers, sold 1,700,000 10-cent stamps, or their equivalent in bonds.

Between July 1, 1941, and June 30, 1946, the Bureau of Engraving and Printing produced more than 8 billion savings stamps of various denominations with a total face value in excess of $1,700,000,000.

The fact that the series E bond became the most widely held security of all time is due in part to the Treasury's encouragement of bond purchases through the payroll savings plan. Some companies had allowed their employees to purchase baby bonds through installment payments taken from their wages, and in 1941 Treasury officials launched a vigorous campaign to persuade business, industry, government, and the military services to make payroll savings plans available for the purchase of E series bonds. Massive drives, using the slogan "everybody every payday," enrolled millions of workers whose purchases were a major source of war bond sales. In 1944, the peak year, bond sales to 27 million participants totaled over $12 billion.

While the Treasury was selling E bonds, it also sold series F and series G savings bonds. Investors could buy F bonds in $25, $100, $500, $1,000, and $10,000 denominations. The bonds, purchased at 74 percent of face value, reached full face value at maturity. Series G bonds, available in denominations of $100, $500, $1,000, $5,000, and $10,000, were purchased at face value and paid interest every six months.

F and G bonds were withdrawn from sale in 1952, but the Treasury continues to sell E bonds through its United States Savings Bonds Division, which is responsible for promoting the sale and retention of the bonds. The division operates with a small headquarters staff in Washington, under the direction of the treasurer of the United States, seven regional offices and field offices in the District of Columbia and in every state except Alaska and North Dakota.

In additon to the series E bond, the Savings Bond Division sells the series H bond. First offered in 1952, the H bond pays interest by Treasury check every six months. Both E and H bonds are registered securities, which means that they will be replaced if lost, stolen, or destroyed.

The United States Savings Bond Division continues to encourage the use of the payroll savings plan, which is responsible for 60 percent of its sales. It also promotes a bond-a-month plan, available at banks. The division relies heavily on the support of volunteers to further bond sales and, as they have in the past, volunteers play a major part in the success of the savings bond program.

Turning out war savings bonds during World War II: The trimming and perforating operation of the Bureau of Engraving and Printing's War Bond section.

President Franklin Roosevelt was photographed on April 30, 1941, as he purchased a defense savings bond from Secretary of the Treasury Henry Morgenthau, Jr., to open the Treasury's defense savings campaign. In a radio broadcast the president urged all Americans to help finance the war against the Axis aggressors.

Movie stars proved to be highly effective bond salesmen. This and the photo on the bottom of the opposite page were taken during a big war bond sales drive.

The 10-cent savings stamp of World War II. Savings stamps, which also came in 25-cent, 50-cent, and $1 denominations, were exchanged for war savings bonds.

During World War II these posters urged Americans to buy war savings bonds and stamps.

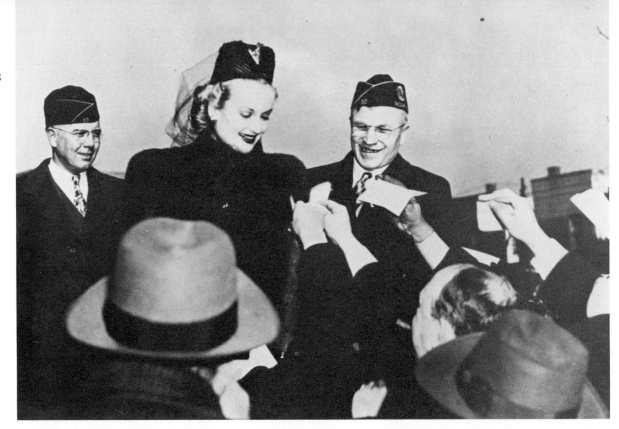

Actress Carole Lombard, pictured here selling bonds to a group of eager buyers, was killed when a plane on which she was returning from a bond drive in Indianapolis, Indiana, crashed into a Nevada mountain in 1942.

Comedians Bud Abbott (second from left) *and Lou Costello* (second from right) *take time out to sell bonds.*

The coaches of this World War II train carried the "Buy Bonds" message.

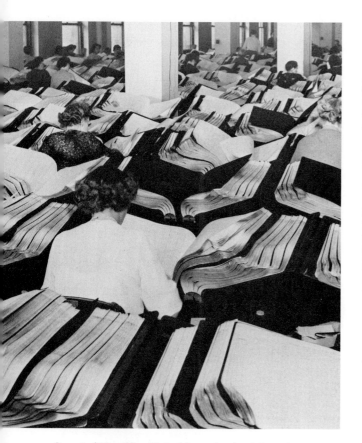

Some 1,400 million United States bond serial numbers were recorded in 2,800 registers, a portion of which are shown here. A blank space opposite each number was reserved for an entry indicating when and where the bond was redeemed. Today the Treasury uses data processing equipment to record and retrieve information about bond ownership.

A group of Hearst newsboys wave the war savings bonds they received as an award for good performance on the job. This photograph was taken on an aircraft carrier.

In 1953 winners of the Voice of Democracy contest were photographed as they watched savings bonds coming off a press at the Bureau of Engraving and Printing.

A payroll savings authorization card which, when filled out and signed, authorizes an employer to withhold a portion of an employee's wages for bond purchases.

(IMPRINT OR TYPE EMPLOYEE'S NAME HERE)   (Dept. or Section)   (Check or Badge Number)

I hereby authorize my employer _____
(Name of company or organization)

to withhold and set apart $_____ from my pay each payday, beginning _____ 19___. When these withholdings equal the cost of the Bond I check here, have Bond issued registered as shown below.

☐ **$50 Bond** Cost $37.50   ☐ **$75 Bond** Cost $56.25   ☐ **$100 Bond** Cost $75.00   ☐ Other Denomination Bond

$25 Bond Cost $18.75
$200 Bond Cost $150
$500 Bond Cost $375

Please register Bonds in this form

OWNER
Mr.
Mrs.
Miss _____ (First) _____ (Middle) _____ (Last) _____ (Social Security No.— See NOTE)

Address: _____
(Street)   (City)   (State)   (Zip)

CO-OWNER ☐ OR BENEFICIARY ☐   (Check only one, if either is desired)
Mr.
Mrs.
Miss _____ (First) _____ (Middle) _____ (Last) _____ (Social Security No.)

NOTE: The owner's Social Security Number must be furnished. If a co-owner or beneficiary is designated, that individual's number, if known, should also be shown. If the latter is a woman, either her title "Miss" or "Mrs." or her Social Security Number must be provided. Married women should use their given names, e.g., "Mrs. Mary J. Smith" not "Mrs. John A. Smith."

This authorization will continue in effect until I advise you to change or cancel it.

IECC/HP 21337 _____ (Date) _____ (Signature of employee-purchaser) _____ SBD-1072

U. S. SAVINGS BONDS PAYROLL SAVINGS AUTHORIZATION

CANVASSER'S REPORT
(Check one and fill in blanks where appropriate)

☐ NEW ENROLLMENT.   AMOUNT OF SAVINGS $_____ EACH PAYDAY.

☐ INCREASE IN PRESENT SAVINGS FROM $_____ TO $_____

☐ CURRENTLY ENROLLED. NO CHANGE IN AMOUNT OF SAVINGS.

☐ CURRENTLY ENROLLED. CHANGE IN BOND DENOMINATION FROM _____ TO _____ .

☐ NOT INTERESTED IN ENROLLING AT THIS TIME.

RETURN THIS CARD TO YOUR DEPARTMENTAL CHAIRMAN AFTER CONTACTING ALL EMPLOYEES ASSIGNED TO YOU.

NECC/HP.19499B

The United States Savings Bonds Division displays these posters to encourage the purchase of bonds.

President Harry S. Truman appears with Secretary of the Treasury Fred M. Vinson at the opening of the Victory Loan drive on October 29, 1945. The objective of the drive, which ran until December 8, 1945, was to raise $11 billion, part of which was to be used for mustering-out pay and care for disabled soldiers and sailors.

In September 1959, President Dwight D. Eisenhower and Secretary of the Treasury Robert Anderson smiled as they announced that the interest rate for series E bonds had been raised to 3 3/4 percent.

Presidential Bond Salesmen

President John F. Kennedy poses with a $25 series E bond.

President Lyndon B. Johnson was urging Americans to use the payroll savings plan to buy bonds when this photo was taken.

President Gerald R. Ford (right) *buys a bond from Secretary of the Treasury William Simon* (center).

In 1909 Secret Service agents surrounded newly inaugurated President William Howard Taft's open carriage during the traditional parade down Pennsylvania Avenue in Washington.

Protecting Presidents and Much More: The United States Secret Service

THE TREASURY'S SECRET SERVICE IS THE OLDEST of the federal government's law enforcement agencies. It was established as a bureau of the Treasury Department in 1865 for the express purpose of controlling the counterfeiters whose activities were destroying the public's confidence in the nation's currency.

During the Civil War years as much as one-third of the paper money in circulation was counterfeit. Approximately sixteen hundred state banks were designing and printing currency and each note carried a different design, making it difficult to distinguish one of the many counterfeit notes from the seven thousand varieties of genuine notes. In 1863 the United States adopted a national currency, issuing the notes that were commonly called greenbacks. But even the national currency was soon counterfeited, and the bogus bills circulated so extensively that the government was compelled to take steps to protect its money. The result was the organization of the United States Secret Service whose agents launched an all-out war on the counterfeiters. Within five years the Secret Service had greatly reduced the amount of counterfeit currency in circulation which, in time, reestablished the integrity of United States notes.

Because it was for many years the principal law enforcement agency of the United States government, the Secret Service received a number of assignments in addition to the suppression of counterfeiting. Secret Service agents investigated espionage cases during the Spanish-American War and during World War I; they investigated frauds in the disposal of public land, the Teapot Dome oil scandal, and the activities of the Ku Klux Klan. But counterfeiters received a major portion of the service's attention and from the beginning its agents were the scourge of the bogus money manufacturers.

One of the Secret Service's early, and most unusual, cases involved Ben Boyd, a notorious counterfeiter, who was arrested and convicted in 1876. He was sent to Joliet Penitentiary in Illinois for ten years, leaving his accomplices, Jack Hughes and Terrence Mullen, with a limited supply of bogus money to pass and with no one to make more. The two, therefore, worked out a bizarre scheme to get Boyd out of prison. They planned to go to the Oak Ridge Cemetery in Springfield, Illinois, the site of President Lincoln's tomb, steal Lincoln's body, and offer it in exchange for Boyd's release from prison.

When Secret Service officials learned of this fantastic plot, they contacted Civil War detective Allan Pinkerton for assistance in dealing with the grave robbers, a type of criminal not customarily investigated by the service. Pinkerton assigned two of his best men to the case.

With the help of the Pinkerton men and the local police, the Secret Service agent in charge worked out a plan designed to catch the grave robbers in the act. On the night of November 7, 1876, the lawmen surrounded the tomb at a distance and waited in the dark. After almost two hours the would-be grave robbers appeared and entered the tomb. With crowbars they managed to move the great stone block that covered the casket. Then, a shot rang out. A detective's percussion cap pistol had fired accidentally, but the other law enforcement officers thought that the robbers were firing at them. They returned the fire and for a moment guns were blazing from several directions. During the confusion Hughes and Mullen escaped into the darkness, but they were caught several days later and ultimately sentenced to a year in prison for attempted grave robbery.

William Brockway, whose career as an active counterfeiter spanned the years 1850 to 1890, appeared many times on the Secret Service's wanted list. One of the most colorful counterfeiters of his generation, he learned the printing trade as a teenage apprentice in New Haven, Connecticut. Before long, Brockway and his elderly employer, whose business was declining, were engaged in a counterfeiting scheme that involved an order from the New Haven City Bank for a supply of $5 notes. As was the custom, the bank president and cashier brought to the printshop the plate and the currency paper to be used. During the printing, Brockway's employer distracted the watchful bankers while the young apprentice made a lead impression of the original $5-note plate. Brockway later produced a copper electrotype from the lead plate, thus obtaining an engraved impression of a $5 bill that was exactly like that on the plate so zealously guarded by the bankers. The counterfeiters printed and passed nearly $100,000 in bogus $5 notes before an alert bank teller noticed a flaw.

After this venture Brockway left New Haven and joined a group of counterfeiters in Hudson, New York. This phase of his career came to an end when he was arrested. He managed to escape, however, and next appeared in Philadelphia where he engaged in various counterfeiting operations. In 1890 the Secret Service arrested the "King of the Counterfeiters" for the last time. Upon his release from prison three years later, Brockway, then seventy-two, as-

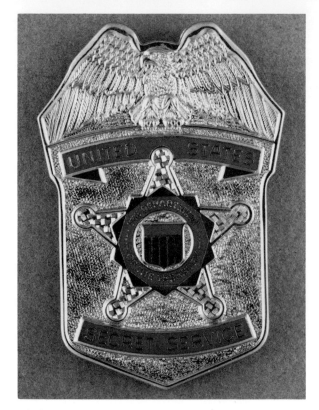

The badge worn by United States Secret Service agents.

sumed the name of Spencer, and for the remaining twenty-seven years of his life stayed clear of the Secret Service, although he was suspected of financing a number of counterfeiting rings. When he died in New Haven, the city where his illegal career began, the "King of the Counterfeiters" was almost a hundred years old.

Emanuel Ninger, alias "Jim the Penman," was another counterfeiter well known to the Secret Service. Ninger, who lived on a small farm in New Jersey, was a sign painter by profession, although he worked infrequently.

Every month Ninger made a trip to New York, leading neighbors to think that he did some investing in the stock market. But the real reason for his trips was to pass counterfeit bills and pick up supplies for making more hand-drawn notes, a unique method of counterfeiting. Ninger made his phony bills by placing a dampened piece of paper on a glass with a genuine note on the opposite side and a strong light beneath. After tracing the design, he finished the counterfeit by sketching with a camel's-hair brush. It was estimated that he turned out between $200 and $300 in hand-drawn counterfeit bills each month, concentrating on $50 and $100 notes.

In March 1896 Ninger made his customary trip to New York. Late in the day, with only one $50 bill

William Brockway as he appeared at the height of his long career as a counterfeiter of government notes and bonds.

Emanuel Ninger, whose hand-drawn counterfeit bills earned him the nickname "Jim the Penman."

left, he went into a saloon and ordered a glass of wine. He asked the owner of the saloon to change the $50 bill. The owner accepted the bill and gave Ninger his change. As Ninger hurried out of the saloon, the owner picked up the $50 bill. When his finger touched the part of the bill that had been lying on the wet bar, some of the ink came off, a sure sign of a counterfeit bill. A saloon employee ran after Ninger, picking up a policeman along the way. They caught up with Ninger and he was arrested. He tried to escape, but was caught again. After lengthy questioning, Ninger revealed the details of his counterfeiting scheme. He received a six-year sentence.

During the fourteen years that Ninger operated he probably distributed some $40,000 worth of his hand-drawn notes, some of which became collector's items. They were, as the *New York Times* put it, "a marvelous piece of work."

William M. Jacobs and William Kendig were Lancaster, Pennsylvania, cigar manufacturers who achieved a distinction unique among counterfeiters by making it necessary for the Treasury to recall an entire issue of currency—$26 million in $100 bills.

With the help of a pair of engravers named Baldwin S. Bredell and Arthur Taylor, Jacobs and Kendig counterfeited cigar tax stamps, which they used to avoid paying the federal tax on the cigars they made. The quartet then decided to try their hand at counterfeiting currency. Taylor had learned to use a new procedure called photoengraving and Bredell had worked out a method for bleaching $1 bills. Using their skills, the engravers printed ninety-seven $100 counterfeit notes on the bleached

$1 bills, and began distributing them.

In December 1897 one of the $100 notes came under suspicion at the subtreasury in Philadelphia. When a few more suspicious bills turned up, they were sent to the Treasury building in Washington for examination. The notes were so good that some officials thought they were genuine. But the Secret Service agents who studied the notes observed that the paper was a little too thick. They placed one in hot water. In seconds, the two split portions of the bleached note, held together with rice paste, separated.

The discovery that such hard-to-detect counterfeits were in circulation caused great alarm in the Treasury Department. The secretary called a press conference to warn the public against the bogus $100 bills, and he also directed Treasury officials to recall the entire issue of genuine $100 bills because the counterfeits looked so much like them.

Meanwhile, the Secret Service began the tedious job of checking on all the engravers in Philadelphia. The list finally narrowed down to Bredell and Taylor whose heavy spending and lack of legitimate work made them obvious suspects. A search of their shop revealed enough to convince Secret Service agents that they had found the makers of the counterfeit $100 bills. Agents followed Taylor to the Lancaster cigar factory, which was placed under a twenty-four-hour surveillance that led to the arrest of Taylor, Bredell, Kendig, and Jacobs.

But that was not the end of the story. In jail, Taylor and Bredell, worried about the severity of their pending sentences, consulted a lawyer who came up with the unusual suggestion that they offer

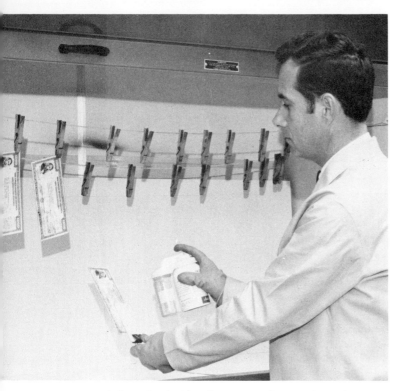

A Secret Service identification specialist uses chemical sprays to develop latent fingerprints, in this case, on forged United States savings bonds. All cases of forgery in the redemption of United States bonds and other securities and government checks are investigated by the Secret Service.

This offset press, with images of counterfeit bills on its rollers, was seized during a raid by Secret Service agents.

to trade counterfeit plates, which they would make in prison, for their freedom.

In those days visitors were not searched and Harry Taylor, Arthur's brother, was able to smuggle into the prison the necessary materials for counterfeiting. The work was done at night, under a blanket, by the light of a small alcohol lamp, which had also been smuggled into the prison. The first step was to photograph the front and back of a genuine $20 note. Lacking a camera, they improvised and made an emulsion from food and other items brought to them. They then split a $20 bill, oiled the two halves, laid the nearly transparent pieces on emulsion-coated metal plates, and produced an outline of the bill's design by holding the plates in the sun's rays at their window. Using their engraving skills, Taylor and Bredell managed to etch the plates, which they used to print bogus $20 bills on 150 new, bleached $1 bills supplied by Harry Taylor.

Five months later, after the printing of the 150 counterfeit $20 bills had been completed, Harry Taylor smuggled the bills and plates out of the

Fingerprints left on counterfeit notes often help to identify those who make and pass them. One of the Secret Service's identification specialists examines bogus notes.

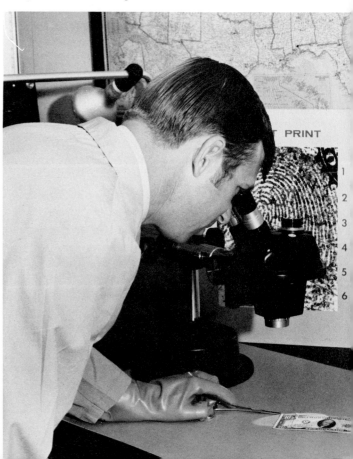

GENUINE

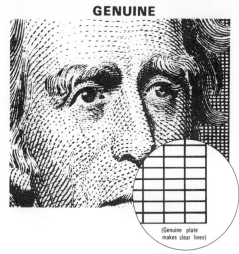

COUNTERFEIT

(Genuine plate makes clear lines)

(Counterfeit plate makes broken lines)

GENUINE PAPER CURRENCY LOOKS GOOD BECAUSE...

IT IS made by experts.
IT IS made on costly machines designed just for that purpose.
IT IS printed from steel plates produced by expert engravers. Genuine engraved plates make clear lines.
IT IS printed on distinctive paper.
IT IS GOOD!

COUNTERFEIT PAPER CURRENCY LOOKS BAD BECAUSE...

IT IS usually a product of inferior workmanship.
IT IS made with equipment designed for other purposes.
IT IS printed from a plate which is made by a photo mechanical process, causing loss of detail.
IT IS printed on paper which does not contain the distinctive red and blue fibers.
IT IS BAD!

PREPARED BY
U.S. SECRET SERVICE

One of the Secret Service's public information releases on detecting counterfeit bills. As part of its war against counterfeiters, the service urges Americans to pay attention to the money they handle.

prison. He buried the plates next to his father's grave and managed to pass thirty-two of the notes before arousing suspicion. He then burned the remainder, but the Secret Service had already entered the case. Agents traced the bogus notes to Harry Taylor and to Arthur Taylor and Baldwin Bredell in prison. The latter two admitted making the plates but claimed to have made them before going to prison. This was disproved, however, because the serial number of the $20 note used as a pattern had not been used on bills until after the pair had entered prison. They tried to bargain for leniency in return for disclosing the location of the plates and testifying against the attorney who planned the counterfeiting scheme. Their offer was refused.

Another counterfeiting case in the Secret Service's files involves an ex-convict named Ralph Brunet, who, in 1963, moved to Frankfurt, Indiana, and began to purchase equipment to operate a printing shop. Because of his suspicious actions, Brunet became the subject of periodic surveillance by Secret Service agents. When it became apparent that the ex-convict was not using his printing equipment for any legitimate purpose, the Secret Service intensified its investigation.

After three months Brunet returned his printing equipment to the supplier, explaining that he was going out of business. When the agents who were following Brunet searched his car, they found $1,370,140 in counterfeit $10 Federal Reserve notes and 194 counterfeit plates in the trunk. The notes represented a record amount to be counterfeited by one individual. The agents arrested Brunet before he could pass any of the notes, which, the counterfeiter claimed, he had worked twelve hours a day for three months to produce. For his efforts he was sentenced to ten years in prison.

Nine men, operating in San Francisco in 1963, produced more than $2 million in counterfeit $20 and $50 Federal Reserve notes, the largest amount known to have been counterfeited at one time within the United States. The group included two tavern owners, a proprietor of a mailing service, three commercial printers, a lithographer, an electronics technician, and a truck driver. Three of the men had prior felony convictions.

The counterfeiters did their photographic work in a small private home rented for that purpose. The plates were made in the offices of the mailing service, and the printing was done in a shop on the Alameda

State College campus, where one of the printers was employed. The counterfeiters returned the notes to the rented house where they used chemicals to give the bogus money an aged appearance. Meanwhile, they began looking for customers among their underworld contacts.

One of the first prospects was an individual who agreed to buy counterfeit notes worth half a million dollars. The customer turned out to be an undercover Secret Service agent and during the transaction, several of the counterfeiters were arrested. The remaining conspirators were apprehended and agents seized $2,237,490 in counterfeit bills. Although the remaining bogus notes turned up in eighteen states, only about $27,000 was actually passed. The counterfeiters received sentences ranging from three months to ten years.

While most counterfeiters confine their activities to the production of bogus currency, there are some, like Rufus Howard Hardin, who specialize in counterfeit United States Treasury checks. Hardin was the ringleader of a group of counterfeiters whose checks began to turn up in Florida, Georgia, Mississippi, Louisiana, and Texas in the spring of 1959. The checks were usually cashed in supermarkets,

Using handwriting specimens from Secret Service files, this special agent hopes to identify the person who forged signatures on stolen United States bonds. During the fiscal year 1974 the Secret Service conducted 13,163 bond-forging investigations and returned an additional 12,383 stolen bonds to their rightful owners before they were redeemed.

Using a device called a coin comparator, a Secret Service expert compares a suspected coin with a genuine one. The corrugated outer edge of a counterfeit coin is often uneven, crooked, or missing altogether.

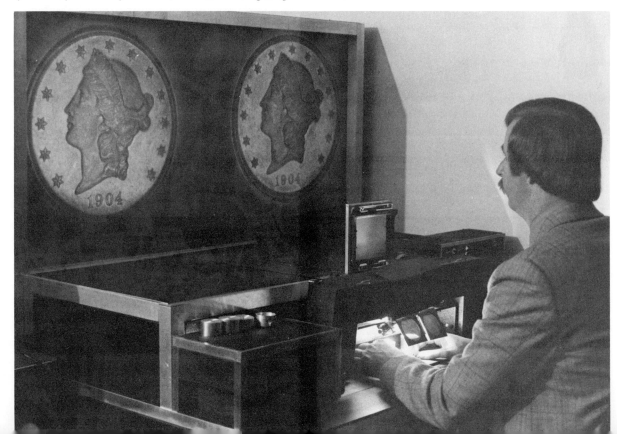

liquor stores, and clothing stores, and the Secret Service had warned merchants and banks to be on the lookout for them.

The first break in the case came when one of the checks was presented at a store in Baton Rouge, Louisiana. Because of the warning from the Secret Service, the check was refused. Moreover, alert sales personnel provided the police with a description of the passer and his car, information that was broadcast on an interstate police network. Two days later Arphy Justin Sonnier was arrested in Beaumont, Texas, and identified as the Baton Rouge passer.

During the intensive investigation that followed, a Secret Service undercover agent operating in Opelousas, Louisiana, made the acquaintance of Louise Roger, Sonnier's girl friend and a suspected member of the conspiracy. The agent, representing himself as a big-time hoodlum from the East cooling off in Louisiana, won her confidence and eventually purchased eleven counterfeit checks from her. The agent then began negotiations for the purchase of checks in quantity, his objective being to reach the leaders of the gang. By this time he had created the impression that he had unlimited funds and major underworld contacts.

At a meeting with the principal distributors of the counterfeit checks, the undercover agent arranged to buy a thousand checks to be delivered, at a price of $20,000, in Washington, D.C. Shortly thereafter, Sonnier, who had been released from police custody, and Louise Roger arrived at Washington National Airport where they were met by the undercover agent and a second agent who was introduced as the party who was backing the purchase of the checks. The delivery was made and the two counterfeiters were arrested. Along with the counterfeit checks, agents seized counterfeit military identification cards, counterfeit Social Security cards, and counterfeit Alabama drivers' licenses.

Because Sonnier and Roger were known to have made trips to Durango, Mexico, the investigation now moved across the border, where Secret Service agents worked with Mexican authorities. A system-

Forged government checks, usually checks that have been stolen from mailboxes, keep Secret Service document analysts busy. Here they compare the signatures on stolen checks with the handwriting of a suspected forger.

atic screening of individuals with the capabilities and facilities for printing counterfeit checks led to two brothers with the reputation of living above their income. A raid on the brothers' printing shop produced the plates for the counterfeit United States Treasury checks, and a general roundup of those involved in the counterfeiting scheme led to the arrest of nine Americans, including the ringleader, Rufus Hardin, and six Mexicans.

In addition to investigating the counterfeiting of United States Treasury checks, the Secret Service also investigates their fraudulent redemption, usually after they have been stolen. One ring of check thieves and forgers, known as the Red Fox Gang, operated briefly in Dallas, Texas. Not satisfied with stolen checks issued for less than $100, the Red Fox Gang altered them by adding the digit "1," thus increasing the amount by $100.

After Treasury checks had been obtained by stealing them from mailboxes and altered with special rubber stamps, a gang member, carrying false iden-

tification, would take a check to a store and ask that it be cashed. If the merchant showed signs of suspicion, another member of the gang, loitering nearby, would greet the passer by name and engage him in conversation. Thus, reassured as to the identity of the person presenting the check, the merchant would cash it.

Within a period of two months the Red Fox Gang stole, altered, and forged some eighty checks, realizing about $7,500 from the operation before nineteen members of the gang were apprehended by the Secret Service acting in cooperation with postal inspectors.

In dealing with both the counterfeiting and fraudulent redemption of Treasury checks, the Secret Service relies on intensive investigation and improved enforcement techniques, but the service also stresses an educational program to inform the public of the methods used by check counterfeiters and forgers.

The Secret Service has been protecting United States presidents since 1901. On September 6 of that year President William McKinley was assassinated while visiting the Pan American Exposition in Buffalo, New York. The assassin, Leon Czolgosz, approached the president in a reception line with a .32-caliber revolver, hidden by a handkerchief, in his right hand. When Czolgosz reached McKinley, he extended his left hand. The president also extended his hand, but Czolgosz pushed it aside and fired his revolver twice. Mortally wounded, McKinley died on September 14. He was the third United States president to be assassinated in thirty-seven years.

In the early days of the nation, there was little concern for the safety of presidents and, consequently, few measures were taken to protect them. On occasion, presidents were the objects of abuse and they received threatening letters. However, as a general rule, they did not take these threats seriously and moved about without protective escorts.

The first serious attempt to assassinate a president occurred on the morning of January 30, 1835, as President Andrew Jackson emerged from the east portico of the Capitol. Richard Lawrence, an English-born house painter, accosted the president and attempted to fire two single-shot brass pistols. Miraculously, both pistols misfired. When the first pistol discharged, Lawrence is said to have been about thirteen feet from the president. On his second attempt, the gun was even closer.

Lawrence was quickly overpowered, arrested, and held for trial. A jury found him not guilty by reason of insanity, and he was confined in jails and mental hospitals for the rest of his life. It is interesting to note that this attack on President Jackson did not inspire any efforts to provide protection for the chief executive.

Abraham Lincoln was the first president to lose his life to an assassin's bullet. The fatal shooting occurred on April 14, 1865, at Ford's Theatre in Washington, where the president was attending a play called *Our American Cousin*. A city policeman had been assigned as the president's bodyguard for the evening. The officer's job was to remain on guard in the corridor outside the presidential box during the entire performance of the play; however, he wandered off and his dereliction of duty left Lincoln unprotected. Consequently, an actor named John Wilkes Booth found his way to the president's box and from a distance of just a few feet shot Lincoln in the head with a single-shot Derringer. The president died the next morning.

Once again, the lack of physical protection for a president resulted in tragedy when James A. Garfield was assassinated in 1881 by Charles J. Guiteau, a disappointed office seeker who had resolved to kill the president.

Guiteau realized his intent on the morning of July 2. As President Garfield walked to a train in the Baltimore and Potomac Railroad Station in Washington, Guiteau stepped forward and from a few feet away shot him in the back with a .44-caliber revolver. At his trial Guiteau testified that he had had three opportunities to shoot the president within a period of three weeks prior to July 2. On each of these occasions the president was unguarded.

After the assassination of President McKinley in 1901, a Secret Service protective detail was provided for Theodore Roosevelt, the former vice-president who became president. However, legislation authorizing presidential protection by the Secret Service was not passed by Congress until 1906.

Members of the first Congress to meet following the death of President McKinley introduced seventeen bills concerning the protection of the president of the United States, but none of them passed. Two proposals for constitutional amendments, one making it treason to kill the president and the other making the assault of the president, or other important federal officials, a federal crime, died in committee. The bill that finally passed was part of the Sundry Civil Expenses Act for 1907. Following the 1908 election, the Secret Service also began protecting the president-elect, a responsibility that was formalized by legislation in 1913.

Legislation passed in 1917 extended Secret Service protection to the members of the president's immediate family, and in 1951 to the vice-president of the United States, upon request. In 1962 Congress authorized the protection of vice-presidents, whether they requested it or not. Protection was also extended to the person next in order of succession to the office of the president, to the vice-president-elect and to past presidents, at their request, for a reasonable period after leaving office.

Meanwhile, there had been a serious attempt on the life of a United States president-elect and another on the life of a president.

> **Protecting the President of the United States**

Secret Service agents, two of whom can be seen in the foreground, keep a watchful eye on the crowd during a public appearance by President Theodore Roosevelt, the first president to receive Secret Service protection.

Here, President Herbert Hoover (center, in top hat) *and his protective escort of Secret Service men are leaving the Capitol after a ceremony.*

Not long after this photo was taken in San Francisco in September 1919, President Woodrow Wilson (standing in car with raised hat) *became ill and had to return to Washington. The three men in the foreground are Secret Service agents.*

Secret Service agents traveled to New York City with President Warren G. Harding on April 19, 1921. The presidential motorcade is seen here leaving Pennsylvania Station en route to the unveiling ceremony for a statue of South American hero Simón Bolivar. Newsreel cameramen in the foreground are recording the president's arrival in New York.

Waving to the crowds, President Franklin Delano Roosevelt rides through Knoxville, Tennessee, on September 9, 1936. Secret Service agents surround the presidential automobile.

The weapons used by Oscar Collazo and Griselio Torresola in their attempt to assassinate President Truman at Blair House in 1950.

Secret Service agents were stationed throughout the crowd at Washington's Griffith Stadium when President Dwight D. Eisenhower threw out the first ball of the 1953 baseball season.

This photograph, taken during a visit by President Harry S. Truman (standing in car) to Muskogee, Oklahoma, includes several vigilant Secret Service men.

At a political rally on the night of February 15, 1933, in Miami's Bayfront Park, President-elect Franklin Delano Roosevelt was the target of an assassin's bullets as he sat atop the rear seat of his car with a small microphone in his hand, making a short informal talk. Fortunately, he slid down into the seat just before Guiseppe Zangara fired five times from a distance of about thirty feet. Zangara's arm was brushed just as he fired and the bullets went wide, striking five other people, wounding four of them and killing Mayor Anton Cermak of Chicago.

After his arrest, Zangara confessed that he had planned to go to Washington to kill President Herbert Hoover, but feared the cold climate would be bad for his stomach trouble. When he learned that President-elect Roosevelt would be in Miami, he resolved to kill him instead.

Although there was no advance warning of the attempt on President Harry S. Truman's life on November 1, 1950, effective protective measures at Blair House (the president's official residence during White House renovation) prevented the assassins from realizing their objective. The assassins, Oscar Collazo and Griselio Torresola, Puerto Rican nationalists living in New York, tried to force their

This photo was taken at a ceremony on December 3, 1963, during which Secretary of the Treasury Douglas Dillon (left) presented to Secret Service Agent Clinton J. Hill an Exceptional Service Award for his bravery in attempting to protect President John F. Kennedy who was assassinated while riding in a motorcade in Dallas, Texas.

way into Blair House, which was guarded by White House policemen and Secret Service agents. In the ensuing gun battle, Torresola and one White House policeman were killed, and Collazo and two White House policemen were wounded. Had the assassins succeeded in entering the front door of Blair House,

President John F. Kennedy's car (left) was followed by two cars carrying Secret Service agents when the president traveled down Pennsylvania Avenue from the Capitol on his Inauguration Day in 1961.

they would probably have been cut down immediately by another Secret Service agent who kept the doorway covered with a submachine gun from his post at the foot of the main stairs. In all, some twenty-seven shots were fired in less than three minutes.

Collazo was brought to trial and sentenced to death, but President Truman commuted the sentence to life imprisonment.

The tragic assassination of President John F. Kennedy brought renewed public attention to the problem of providing protection for the chief executive of the United States and other high-ranking officials. On November 22, 1963, President Kennedy ws shot and killed by a sniper while riding in a motorcade in Dallas, Texas. Shots fired by the sniper, alleged to be Lee Harvey Oswald, also wounded Texas Governor John B. Connally. In a bizarre turn of events, Oswald was himself shot and killed two days later.

One result of President Kennedy's assassination was a law, passed in 1965, making it a federal violation to assassinate, kidnap, or assault the president of the United States, the president-elect, the vice-president, or the person next in order of succession to the office of the president of the United States, the vice-president-elect, or any individual acting as pres-

Crowds along the parade route on Inauguration Day in 1973 are kept under surveillance by the Secret Service agents protecting President Richard Nixon.

ident under the Constitution and the laws of the United States. Another 1965 act extended Secret Service protection to a former president and his wife during his lifetime. In 1968 the Secret Service was authorized to provide protection for the widow of a former president until her death or remarriage. The 1968 legislation also provided for the protection of

Secret Service men walk beside President Lyndon B. Johnson's car during a motorcade through a Pittsburgh suburb.

Secret Service agents are clearing a path for President Gerald R. Ford.

On Inauguration Day in 1977 four Secret Service men were assigned to the car carrying Vice-President and Mrs. Walter Mondale.

This photo of the presidential reviewing stand was taken while the 1977 inaugural parade was in progress. President and Mrs. Jimmy Carter are seated in the front row at the left. The man in the foreground is a Secret Service agent.

Under the watchful eyes of several Secret Service agents, President Carter (center) and Vice-President Mondale (at the president's left) greet well-wishers near Blair House, the presidential guest house.

President Carter (left) *and Vice-President Mondale* (on the president's left) *are accompanied by four Secret Service agents as they walk along a Washington street.*

minor children of a former president until age sixteen, and other legislation directed the Secret Service to protect major presidential and vice-presidential candidates.

Additional legislation expanding Secret Service responsibilities became law in 1970 when President Richard Nixon signed a bill establishing the Executive Protective Service. It replaced the White House Police, a uniformed police force under the supervision of the Secret Service that had, since 1922, guarded the White House grounds and protected the president and his family while they were in residence at the Executive Mansion. The Executive Protective Service is also under the supervision of the Secret Service and, in addition to guarding the White House and its occupants, its uniformed officers provide security at buildings in which presidential offices are located and at foreign diplomatic missions in Washington and in other areas, at the direction of the president. The Executive Protective Service is also charged with protecting the vice-president and his immediate family and the vice-president's official residence in Washington.

Executive Protective Service officers have the same privileges and powers as members of Washington's police force. They carry out their protective responsibilities from fixed guard posts and by means of foot and vehicular patrols.

Like the Executive Protective Service, the Treasury Police Force is a uniformed security unit of the Secret Service. Its members protect the Treasury building and annex and the millions of dollars in securities and currency that they house. Police Force officers are stationed at the entrances to the Treasury building to check on visitors and whatever packages they may be carrying. Members of the Police Force have the power to arrest persons who violate laws within the building and they investigate crimes committed there.

In 1971 the United States extended the protection of its Secret Service to the visiting heads of foreign governments, other distinguished visitors to the United States, and to official representatives of the United States performing special missions abroad.

Secret Service protective measures are, for the most part, uniform for all persons in its care, whether the protectee is the president on a trip away from the White House or a distinguished guest of the United States. Preparations begin with the assigning of an agent to plan security details, who, with his staff, works with the agent in charge of the Secret Service's district field office in the area to be visited. In many cases more than one field office will be involved.

From advance security surveys, Secret Service agents determine the manpower and equipment that will be required for adequate protection. They also note the location of hospitals, evacuation routes, and other emergency sites. Before the visit agents conduct briefings to inform all those involved of their assignments, where they will be posted, and what is expected of them on post. The briefings also include a rundown on the identification that will be worn by all participants, contingency plans in the event of an emergency, and protective intelligence information, some of the latter coming from law enforcement and intelligence agencies that have files on individuals or groups that might pose a threat to the person being protected. Security during the actual visit is controlled from a command post, which directs the mission and reports as well as receives information.

From time to time the Secret Service has been called upon to protect priceless documents and other objects of great value. In December 1941, Secret Service agents guarded the Declaration of Independence, the Constitution of the United States, the Gutenberg Bible, Lincoln's Second Inaugural Address, and the Lincoln Cathedral copy of the Magna Carta when these famous documents were taken from the Library of Congress in Washington to a place of safety for the duration of World War II. They were escorted back to Washington by the Secret Service at the war's end.

Secret Service agents also protected the United Nations Charter when it was moved in April 1945 from San Francisco to the State Department in Washington and, at the request of President Kennedy, they safeguarded the Mona Lisa by Leonardo da Vinci during its exhibition in the United States in 1962 and 1963.

Today, more than a century after the first Secret Service agents began to track down the counterfeiters whose activities were undermining the value of United States currency, the primary responsibility of the Secret Service is the protection of presidents and other ranking officials. However, as the federal government's protective agency and one of its most important investigative arms, the Secret Service continues to protect the nation's money and to perform other law enforcement duties at the request of Congress and the president of the United States.

When this photo was taken in 1951, the then Princess Elizabeth of England (in first car) was visiting Washington. A car containing Secret Service agents follows the one in which the princess is riding.

An Executive Protective Service officer on duty at the north portico of the White House.

Executive Protective Service officers at one of the entrances to the White House grounds.

These Protective Service officers, assigned to the Service's Foreign Missions Division, are on duty (left) at the embassy of Japan and (right) at the embassy of Iran.

Two members of the Treasury Police Force pose at the entrance to a Treasury vault. Among other duties, Police Force officers clear the two thousand employees and three thousand visitors who enter the Treasury building each day.

Forty hours of firearms training is required of all recruits attending the center's Criminal Investigator and Police schools. This photo was taken during target practice on an indoor range.

A School for Federal Agents: The Federal Law Enforcement Training Center

At a former naval base in Glynco, Georgia, the Treasury Department operates a facility that provides a good example of how diverse its activities are. The facility is the Federal Law Enforcement Training Center where the Treasury schools its own law enforcement agents and agents from other government departments. All the trainees are preparing for jobs that involve the power of arrest and the authority to carry arms.

The Federal Law Enforcement Training Center was established in 1970 by the Treasury with the cooperation of several federal agencies with law enforcement responsibilities. Previously, the Treasury had provided training for its own people at its Treasury Law Enforcement School; other government agencies involved in law enforcement operated similar schools. Today, at a considerable saving to the taxpayer, the Federal Law Enforcement Training Center serves twenty-nine federal agencies representing ten executive departments.

At Glynco the training received by a student depends on his previous experience and on the skills he will need as a special agent or police officer of his particular agency. The center offers a basic course that is required for all recruits, and refresher, advanced, and specialized courses for agents and police officers who already have some experience on the job. Courses for recruits and courses for students from more than one

agency are taught by instructors employed by the center. Specialized courses for recruits and advanced courses for students from a single agency are taught by instructors supplied by the agency involved. The Treasury Department provides the facilities and equipment for all the courses taught at Glynco.

Most of the Federal Law Enforcement Training Center's students are recruits and for them the center conducts a Criminal Investigator Training Division and a Police Training Division. The Criminal Investigator Division provides initial training for newly recruited special agents, including the men and women who will serve as agents for the Treasury Department's law enforcement agencies: the Bureau of Alcohol, Tobacco and Firearms, the United States Customs Service, the Internal Revenue Service, and the United States Secret Service. The Police Division provides basic recruit training for uniformed and other police officers from the Treasury's Executive Protective Service; the Department of the Interior's National Park Service, Bureau of Indian Affairs, and Fish and Wildlife Service; the Department of Justice's Immigration and Naturalization Service; the Agricultural Department's Forest Service, and other agencies.

During an eight-week course, the center's Criminal Investigator Division gives instruction in about fifty different areas of law enforcement. Students

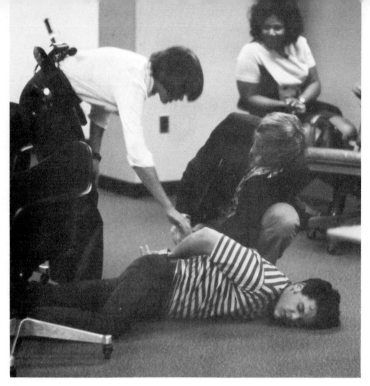

Proper methods of search and seizure are the subjects of a class-room demonstration.

learn how to conduct surveillance, how to interview suspects, how to make raids and arrests, and how to testify in court. They also study hand-to-hand defensive techniques, although the center offers no instruction in karate or judo. As part of their training in the use of firearms, students must achieve a qualifying score (at least 210 out of a possible 300) on an

While their fellow recruits watch, two students at the Federal Law Enforcement Training Center practice what they have learned about disarming a suspect.

indoor target range. They also train on an outdoor target range.

Students learn how to conduct a successful surveillance by actually following an experienced agent who is acting the part of a suspect. Aided by a description and a photograph of the suspect, the trainee shadows him, noting where he goes and what he does. Later the student reports on his surveillance to his classmates. The subject of the surveillance also appears before the class to point out errors made by the trainee.

Students learn good interviewing techniques by questioning instructors who are playing the roles of suspects or witnesses to a crime. While the trainee attempts to obtain information that will help solve his case, his success, or lack of it, is recorded on video tape for subsequent study in class.

Trainees also learn how to conduct successful raids by participating in simulations of the real thing. A team of students may visit an apartment whose occupants are under suspicion. In the course of the raid they will be confronted with distractions, such as an attorney who demands admission, to which they must make an appropriate response. Or the students may take part in an outdoor raid exercise that requires them to use natural surroundings for concealment and mobile equipment for communications. Practice raids teach the students the importance of teamwork and test their ability to react effectively to fast-moving events.

The Federal Law Enforcement Training Center's Police Division course, which lasts twelve weeks, provides basic instruction in about forty subjects related to general police work. In addition to studying criminal conduct, organized crime, fingerprinting, and other subjects in the classroom, students fire weapons on indoor and outdoor ranges and take part in simulated raids.

Federal Law Enforcement Training Center students come from all parts of the United States. Each participating agency establishes its own qualifications for sending trainees to the center. When there is space, trainees from state or local law enforcement agencies are admitted, but the center's curriculum concentrates on law enforcement activities on the federal level.

These center students are learning how to use radio equipment to communicate with other agents and with command posts.

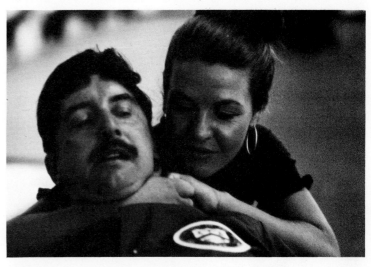

During their recruit training, students at the center master the basic techniques of self-defense.

A practice narcotics raid was under way when this photo was taken.

Recruits were studying arrest procedures when this photo was taken.

These students are learning by doing as they participate in a practice arrest.

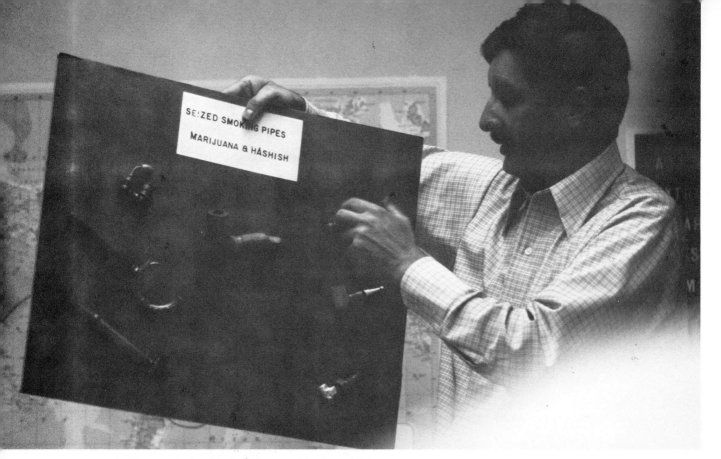

An instructor is describing equipment used by drug addicts.

A recruit fires on an outdoor range.

Because federal officers may have to deal with protests and other disturbances, crowd control is part of the Federal Law Enforcement Training Center curriculum.

Secretaries of the Treasury/ Treasurers of the United States

Secretaries of the Treasury

Secretaries	Term of Service From	Term of Service To	Presidents
1. Alexander Hamilton, New York	Sept. 11, 1789	Jan. 31, 1795	Washington
2. Oliver Wolcott, Connecticut	Feb. 3, 1795	Mar. 3, 1797	
Oliver Wolcott, Connecticut	Mar. 4, 1797	Dec. 31, 1800	Adams, John
3. Samuel Dexter, Massachussets	Jan. 1, 1801	Mar. 3, 1801	
Samuel Dexter, Massachusetts	Mar. 4, 1801	May 13, 1801	Jefferson
4. Albert Gallatin, Pennsylvania	May 14, 1801	Mar. 3, 1809	
Albert Gallatin, Pennsylvania	Mar. 4, 1809	Feb. 8, 1814	Madison
5. George W. Campbell, Tennessee	Feb. 9, 1814	Oct. 5, 1814	
6. Alexander J. Dallas, Pennsylvania	Oct. 6, 1814	Oct. 21, 1816	
7. William H. Crawford, Georgia	Oct. 22, 1816	Mar. 3, 1817	
William H. Crawford, Georgia	Mar. 4, 1817	Mar. 6, 1825	Monroe
8. Richard Rush, Pennsylvania	Mar. 7, 1825	Mar. 5, 1829	Adams, J. Q.
9. Samuel D. Ingham, Pennsylvania	Mar. 6, 1829	June 20, 1831	Jackson
10. Louis McLane, Delaware	Aug. 8, 1831	May 28, 1833	
11. Wm. J. Duane, Pennsylvania	May 29, 1833	Sept. 22, 1833	
12. Roger B. Taney, Maryland	Sept. 23, 1833	June 25, 1834	
13. Levi Woodbury, New Hampshire	July 1, 1834	Mar. 3, 1837	
Levi Woodbury, New Hampshire	Mar. 4, 1837	Mar. 3, 1841	Van Buren
14. Thomas Ewing, Ohio	Mar. 6, 1841	Apr. 4, 1841	Harrison
Thomas Ewing, Ohio	Apr. 5, 1841	Sept. 11, 1841	Tyler
15. Walter Forward, Pennsylvania	Sept. 13, 1841	Mar 1, 1843	
16. John C. Spencer, New York	Mar. 8, 1843	May 2, 1844	
17. George M. Bibb, Kentucky	July 4, 1844	Mar. 4, 1845	
George M. Bibb, Kentucky	Mar. 5, 1845	Mar. 7, 1845	Polk
18. Robert J. Walker, Mississippi	Mar. 8, 1845	Mar. 5, 1849	

Secretaries of the Treasury—Continued

Secretaries	Term of Service From	Term of Service To	Presidents
19. Wm. M. Meredith, Pennsylvania	Mar. 8, 1849	July 9, 1850	Taylor
Wm. M. Meredith, Pennsylvania	July 10, 1850	July 22, 1850	Fillmore
20. Thomas Corwin, Ohio	July 23, 1850	Mar. 6, 1853	
21. James Guthrie, Kentucky	Mar. 7, 1853	Mar. 6, 1857	Pierce
22. Howell Cobb, Georgia	Mar. 7, 1857	Dec. 8, 1860	Buchanan
23. Philip F. Thomas, Maryland	Dec. 12, 1860	Jan. 14, 1861	
24. John A. Dix, New York	Jan. 15, 1861	Mar. 6, 1861	
25. Salmon P. Chase, Ohio	Mar. 7, 1861	June 30, 1864	Lincoln
26. Wm. P. Fessenden, Maine	July 5, 1864	Mar. 3, 1865	
27. Hugh McCulloch, Indiana	Mar. 9, 1865	Apr. 15, 1865	
Hugh McCulloch, Indiana	Apr. 16, 1865	Mar. 3, 1869	Johnson, A.
28. Geo. S. Boutwell, Massachusetts	Mar. 12, 1869	Mar. 16, 1873	Grant
29. Wm. A. Richardson, Massachusetts	Már. 17, 1873	June 3, 1874	
30. Benjamin H. Bristow, Kentucky	June 4, 1874	June 20, 1876	
31. Lot M. Morrill, Maine	June 7, 1876	Mar. 3, 1877	
Lot M. Morrill, Maine	Mar. 4, 1877	Mar. 9, 1877	Hayes
32. John Sherman, Ohio	Mar. 10, 1877	Mar. 3, 1881	
33. William Windom, Minnesota	Mar. 8, 1881	Sept. 19, 1881	Garfield
William Windom, Minnesota	Sept. 20, 1881	Nov. 13, 1881	Arthur
34. Charles J. Folger, New York	Nov. 14, 1881	Sept. 4, 1884	
35. Walter Q. Gresham, Indiana	Sept. 25, 1884	Oct. 30, 1884	
36. *Hugh McCulloch, Indiana	Oct. 31, 1884	Mar. 3, 1885	
Hugh McCulloch, Indiana	Mar. 4, 1885	Mar. 7, 1885	Cleveland
37. Daniel Manning, New York	Mar. 8, 1885	Mar. 31, 1887	
38. Charles S. Fairchild, New York	Apr. 1, 1887	Mar. 3, 1889	
Charles S. Fairchild, New York	Mar. 4, 1889	Mar. 6, 1889	Harrison, B.
39. *William Windom, Minnesota	Mar. 7, 1889	Jan. 29, 1891	
40. Charles Foster, Ohio	Feb. 25, 1891	Mar. 3, 1893	
Charles Foster, Ohio	Mar. 4, 1893	Mar. 6, 1893	Cleveland
41. John G. Carlisle, Kentucky	Mar. 7, 1893	Mar. 3, 1897	
John G. Carlisle, Kentucky	Mar. 4, 1897	Mar. 5, 1897	McKinley
42. Lyman J. Gage, Illinois	Mar. 6, 1897	Sept. 14, 1901	
Lyman J. Gage, Illinois	Sept. 15, 1901	Jan. 31, 1902	Roosevelt, T.
43. L. M. Shaw, Iowa	Feb. 1, 1902	Mar. 3, 1907	
44. G. B. Cortelyou, New York	Mar. 4, 1907	Mar. 7, 1909	
45. Franklin MacVeagh, Illinois	Mar. 8, 1909	Mar. 5, 1913	Taft
46. W. G. McAdoo, New York	Mar. 6, 1913	Dec. 15, 1918	Wilson
47. Carter Glass, Virginia	Dec. 16, 1918	Feb. 1, 1920	
48. David F. Houston, Missouri	Feb. 2, 1920	Mar. 3, 1921	

* Indicates nonsequential second appointment by a later Administration.

| Secretaries | Term of Service | | Presidents |
	From	To	
49. Andrew W. Mellon, Pennsylvania	Mar. 4, 1921	Aug. 2, 1923	Harding
Andrew W. Mellon, Pennsylvania	Aug. 3, 1923	Mar. 3, 1929	Coolidge
Andrew W. Mellon, Pennsylvania	Mar. 4, 1929	Feb. 12, 1932	Hoover
50. Ogden L. Mills, New York	Feb. 13, 1932	Mar. 4, 1933	
51. William H. Woodin, New York	Mar. 5, 1933	Dec. 31, 1933	Roosevelt, F. D.
52. Henry Morgenthau, Jr., New York	Jan. 1, 1934	Apr. 12, 1945	
Henry Morgenthau, Jr., New York	Apr. 13, 1945	July 22, 1945	Truman
53. Fred M. Vinson, Kentucky	July 23, 1945	June 23, 1946	
54. John W. Snyder, Missouri	June 25, 1946	Jan. 20, 1953	
55. George M. Humphrey, Ohio	Jan. 21, 1953	July 29, 1957	Eisenhower
56. Robert B. Anderson, Connecticut	July 29, 1957	Jan. 20, 1961	
57. Douglas Dillon, New Jersey	Jan. 21, 1961	Apr. 1, 1965	Kennedy Johnson, L. B.
58. Henry H. Fowler, Virginia	Apr. 1, 1965	Dec. 20, 1968	Johnson, L. B.
59. Joseph W. Barr, Indiana	Dec. 21, 1968	Jan. 20, 1969	
60. David M. Kennedy, Utah	Jan. 22, 1969	Feb. 10, 1971	Nixon
61. John B. Connally, Texas	Feb. 11, 1971	June 12, 1972	
62. George P. Shultz, Illinois	June 12, 1972	May 8, 1974	
63. William E. Simon, New Jersey	May 8, 1974	Jan. 17, 1977	Nixon Ford
64. W. Michael Blumenthal, Michigan	Jan. 21, 1977		Carter

Treasurers of the United States

Name	Whence Appointed	Date of Commission	Expiration of Service
1. Michael Hillegas ....Pennsylvania ....July 29, 1775 .....Sept. 11, 1789
2. Samuel Meredith ....Pennsylvania ....Sept. 11, 1789 .....Oct. 31, 1801
3. Thomas T. Tucker ....South Carolina ....Dec. 1, 1801 ......May 2, 1828
4. William Clark ....Pennsylvania ....June 4, 1828 ......May 31, 1829
5. John Campbell ....Virginia ....May 26, 1829 ......July 20, 1839
6. William Selden ....Virginia ....July 22, 1839 .....Nov. 23, 1850
7. John Sloan ....Ohio ....Nov. 27, 1850 .....April 6, 1852
8. Samuel Casey ....Kentucky ....April 4, 1853 ......Dec. 22, 1859
9. William C. Price ....Missouri ....Feb. 28, 1860 .....Mar. 21, 1861
10. F E. Spinner ....New York ....Mar. 16, 1861 .....June 30, 1875
11. John C. New ....Indiana ....June 30, 1875 .....July 1, 1876
12. A. U. Wyman ....Wisconsin ....July 1, 1876 ......June 30, 1877
13. James Gilfillan ....Connecticut ....July 1, 1877 ......Mar. 31, 1883
14. A. U. Wyman ....Wisconsin ....April 1, 1883 .....April 30, 1885
15. Conrad N. Jordan ....New York ....May 1, 1885 .....May 23, 1887

Treasurers of the United States

Name	Whence Appointed	Date of Commission	Expiration of Service
16. James W. Hyatt	Connecticut	May 24, 1887	May 10, 1889
17. J. N. Huston	Indiana	May 11, 1889	April 24, 1891
18. Enos H. Nebecker	Indiana	April 25, 1891	May 31, 1893
19. D. N. Morgan	Connecticut	June 1, 1893	June 30, 1897
20. Ellis H. Roberts	New York	July 1, 1897	June 30, 1905
21. Chas. H. Treat	New York	July 1, 1905	Oct. 30, 1909
22. Lee McClung	Tennessee	Nov. 1, 1909	Nov. 21, 1912
23. Carmi A. Thompson	Ohio	Nov. 22, 1912	Mar. 31, 1913
24. John Burke	North Dakota	April 1, 1913	Jan. 5, 1921
25. Frank White	North Dakota	May 2, 1921	May 1, 1928
26. H. T. Tate	Tennessee	May 31, 1928	Jan. 17, 1929
27. W. O. Woods	Kansas	Jan. 18, 1929	May 31, 1933
28. W. A. Julian	Ohio	June 1, 1933	May 29, 1949

After the death of Treasurer W. A. Julian, Michael E. Slindee, Deputy and Acting Treasurer, served under Presidential authority from May 29, 1949 to June 21, 1949.

Name	Whence Appointed	Date of Commission	Expiration of Service
29. Georgia Neese Clark	Kansas	June 21, 1949	Jan. 27, 1953
30. Ivy Baker Priest	Utah	Jan. 28, 1953	Jan. 29, 1961
31. Elizabeth Rudel Smith	California	Jan. 30, 1961	April 13, 1962

Upon Treasurer Smith's resignation, William T. Howell, Deputy Treasurer, was designated to serve as Acting Treasurer of the United States until the appointment of a successor to Mrs. Smith.

Name	Whence Appointed	Date of Commission	Expiration of Service
32. Kathryn O'Hay Granahan	Pennsylvania	Jan. 3, 1963	Nov. 20, 1966

Upon Treasurer Granahan's resignation, William T. Howell, Deputy Treasurer, was designated to serve as Acting Treasurer of the United States until the appointment of a successor to Mrs. Granahan.

Name	Whence Appointed	Date of Commission	Expiration of Service
33. Dorothy Andrews Elston	Delaware	May 8, 1969	

Upon Treasurer Elston's marriage to Walter L. Kabis, on September 17, 1970, her name officially became Dorothy Andrews Kabis.

Name	Whence Appointed	Date of Commission	Expiration of Service
Dorothy Andrews Kabis	Delaware		July 3, 1971

Upon Treasurer Kabis' death, William T. Howell, Deputy Treasurer, was designated to serve as Acting Treasurer of the United States until the appointment of a successor to Mrs. Kabis.

Name	Whence Appointed	Date of Commission	Expiration of Service
34. Romana Acosta Banuelos	California	Dec. 17, 1971	Feb. 14, 1974 (Resigned)
35. Francine Irving Neff	New Mexico	June 21, 1974	Jan. 19, 1977
36. Azie T. Morton	Virginia	Sept. 12, 1977	

Index

Italicized numbers indicate illustrations